The Best
Stage Scenes
of 1997

Other books by Jocelyn A. Beard

100 Men's Stage Monologues from the 1980s

100 Women's Stage Monologues from the 1980s

The Best Men's/Women's Stage Monologues of 1990

The Best Men's/Women's Stage Monologues of 1991

The Best Men's/Women's Stage Monologues of 1992

The Best Men's/Women's Stage Monologues of 1993

The Best Men's/Women's Stage Monologues of 1994

The Best Men's/Women's Stage Monologues of 1995

The Best Men's/Women's Stage Monologues of 1996

The Best Men's/Women's Stage Monologues of 1997

The Best Stage Scenes for Men from the 1980s

The Best Stage Scenes for Women from the 1980s

The Best Stage Scenes of 1992

The Best Stage Scenes of 1993

The Best Stage Scenes of 1994

The Best Stage Scenes of 1995

The Best Stage Scenes of 1996

Monologues from Classic Plays 468 B.C. to 1960 A.D.

Scenes from Classic Plays 468 B.C. to 1970 A.D.

100 Great Monologues from the Renaissance Theatre

100 Great Monologues from the Neo-Classical Theatre

100 Great Monologues from the 19th C. Romantic & Realistic Theatres

The Best
Stage Scenes
of 1997

edited by Jocelyn A. Beard

SCENE STUDY SERIES

A SMITH AND KRAUS BOOK

Published by Smith and Kraus, Inc.
One Main Street, Lyme, NH 03768

Copyright © 1998 by Smith and Kraus, Inc.
All rights reserved
Manufactured in the United States of America

First Edition: December 1998
10 9 8 7 6 5 4 3 2 1

The Scene Study Series 1067-3253

NOTE: These scenes are intended to be used for audition and class study; permission is not required to use the material for those purposes. However, if there is a paid performance of any of the scenes included in this book, please refer to the permissions acknowledgment pages to locate the source who can grant permission for public performance.

Contents

WOMEN'S SCENES

MEN'S SCENES

Forword

○ ○ ○

Good scenes are not—as some would have you believe—a dime a dozen. They don't grow on trees. They aren't free for the taking. Most playwrights go out of their way to ensure their opus contains at least one kick-ass monologue. Fewer these days concentrate on the structure of their scenes. As the form of theatrical writing shifts and evolves, it becomes a bit of a challenge to fill this yearly volume with material that I know will offer opportunities to actors to hone their craft as well as appealing to the lay persons who utilize these books to stay au courant with what's hot on the boards.

1997 was an exhausting year in theatre. There was an avalanche of great new work from new voices as well as old. This book contains 40 scenes that showcase some of the year's most compelling theatrical storytelling and should fulfill your need for scenes to work with until next year.

As always: if you find something you like, read the play! There's nothing like it.

Break a leg.

Jocelyn Beard
Patterson, NY
Summer, 1997

This book is dedicated to my good pal, Nannette Stone.

MEN'S AND WOMEN'S SCENES

ALKI

A version of Ibsen's *Peer Gynt* Set in the Pacific Northwest and points south, drawn freehand and writ large by Eric Overmeyer

Man & Woman
Peer (20's) a wiry, raggedy youth and Hannah (40's) his scolding mother.

Scene: the Puget Sound Territory, 1851

> *Here, the rascally Peer does his best to spin an elaborate tale of personal heroism for his disbelieving mother.*

○ ○ ○

The Puget Sound Territory, 1851. Tall trees. Endless forest. A cold & rocky shore. An overcast summer day. Peer, a wiry, raggedy youth of twenty, appears, followed by his scolding mother, Hannah Gynt.

HANNAH GYNT: Liar!

PEER: Ain't!

HANNAH GYNT: Lies, lies, more lies, and damn lies, salted over with stretchers for seasoning, and pure unadulterated whoppers for dessert.

PEER: Honest, Ma, I swear.

HANNAH GYNT: Don't swear, son. Your nose is getting longer by the minute, and your eyes is turning dark dark brown.

PEER: Every word true, so help me Jesus.

HANNAH GYNT: Now you've done it. Taking God's name. Well go ahead. Tell it again. See if we ain't struck dead by lightning right here in broad daylight. Tell me how you been gone six long weeks, and come home empty-handed, clothes in tatters and lost your rifle, and nothing to show for your meanderings but a mouthful of outlandish foolishness, and us with no more 'n a thimbleful of dried salmonberries in the larder and winter already whispering in the wind and the wolf scratching at the door. Go ahead, tell it. See if I believe you this time.

PEER: Happened just like I said. I hiked all the way to Mount Tahoma—

HANNAH GYNT: That's more 'n ninety mile—

PEER: Took me a week of hard walking, too, and never mind the weather, nor the shoe leather, nor the mosquitoes, neither. Skeeters so big they could stand flat-footed and consummate the vows of Holy Matrimony with full-grown wild turkeys. So there I was, beset on all sides by hostile elements and nature red in tooth and claw. Living on nothing but wild berries, and salmon from the streams, which I caught with my bare hands like a grizzly bear, just swooped 'em out of the water like that!

HANNAH GYNT: Goodness gracious. And I suppose you ate them salmon raw—

PEER: Don't be silly, Ma, I had my flint. Why even in a howling rainstorm, when the drops are sharp 'n hard 'n sideways like bullets, I can conjure a fire that'll make the Devil take off his shoes and warm his feet.

HANNAH GYNT: His cloven feet—

PEER: His cloven feet.

HANNAH GYNT: And then? Where'd you spy this mighty buck?

PEER: I'm getting to that. I hiked for days towards Mount Tahoma. Through forest, marsh and meadow. And I seen lots of game. Deer and badger and elk. But I let 'em go undisturbed.

HANNAH GYNT: Did you? That's kindhearted of you, and us near starving to death with not two copper pennies to rub together since your no-good wastrel father took off like a thief in the night with what was left of my daddy's money, after he'd drunk up or gambled or whored most of it away—

PEER: Ma, that was fifteen years ago—

HANNAH GYNT: And still sticks in my craw every time I think

4 men's and women's scenes

about it. So tell me again why you disdained to harvest the providential bounty all around you?

PEER: I knew what I was looking for, and weren't about to waste my powder on the paltry, puny, and pecunious. And there in the forests of the foothills of Mount Tahoma, I found him.

HANNAH GYNT: The buck—

PEER: The most magnificent buck you ever seen, Ma. Tall at the shoulder as two men. Broad across as a river in spring flood. And antlers like the King of Poland's good-time chandelier. Must've been thirty points on that head, prob'ly more.

HANNAH GYNT: I ain't never seen a buck that size—

PEER: Nor me neither, not 'til now. I swear, Ma, this creature was bigger 'n Paul Bunyan's blue ox, Babe. By half—

HANNAH GYNT: (Drawn in.) Gracious. So you really seen him, after all. Then what happened?

PEER: He looked at me, and I looked at him, and I swung my rifle up and pulled the hammer back, and at the sound he lit out for the mountaintop, leaping from ridge to ridge faster 'n a greased pig at a Swedish roof raiser. And I let loose with a shot that not one man in a thousand could have made.

HANNAH GYNT: Missed him completely, I 'spect.

PEER: No, m'am. I got him, alright. Caught him on the fly as he was taking the next ridge in a single bound. Dead center, through the shoulder, under the rib cage, and nicked his heart. That was some shot, if I do say so myself. Like clipping the wings off a baby hummingbird at a hundred yards.

HANNAH GYNT: And so he dropped like a gutshot duck, did he?

PEER: No m'am. That buck was so big and so strong, he barely flinched. Just kept flying up the mountain, leaping from rock to rock like the biggest mountain goat you ever seen. And I'm running after him, best as I can, picking out his trail by climbing a couple hundred feet up into the trees every mile or so to find a broken twig or a trace of blood, where he'd gone flying by.

HANNAH GYNT: A flying buck, if that don't beat all. Oh I wish I could've seen that!

PEER: Oh, he was something alright. I tracked him through that trackless forest for three days and three nights, the trees so big they blotted out the sun, so I couldn't tell what time of day it was, and the weather up top completely different from the weather on the ground, snowing one place and raining the other, and that buck moving so fast I didn't dare stop to eat or sleep, just lived on berries snatched along the way, and some morning dew as I could suck from the very air—tracked him all the way around the base of Mount Tahoma, must've been a hundred miles, easy, and he couldn't shake me, try as he might. So then he started up the mountain, and by the fifth day he wasn't flying no more, just walking, but still moving pretty strong, straight up the mountain, across glaciers and icefields and old lava flows and fields of vertical scree, and there wasn't nary a handhold or a place for a person to put his feet, and many's the time I thought I was gonna lose my grip and fall a thousand feet straight down and end up dead and lonesome on some godforsaken pile of broken rock—

HANNAH GYNT: But you didn't. Thank heavens—

PEER: No, m'am. I didn't. I kept my footing, and I kept my resolve, and I tracked that buck up hill and over dale and all the way to the top of Mount Tahoma. And there I stood at the very apex of the world, smack dab in the middle of the Good Lord's bountiful Creation, and I could see all the way to California the other, and I could see the great Pacific Ocean shining in the distance, and China on the horizon—

HANNAH GYNT: China! My word! Was it upside down?

PEER: Not the part I could make out. Looked plumb right-side up to me. And I could see the Columbia and the Snake rolling down to the sea all silvery, and where Paul Bunyan and Babe the Blue Ox carved out Puget Sound and made the Cascades with what dirt and stone was left over from their mighty excavation—

HANNAH GYNT: And what about the buck, son? What about the poor buck? Mortally wounded and failing fast—

6 men's and women's scenes

PEER: Oh, as I was busy admiring this vista, which prob'ly no white man had ever seen before, he slipped down the other side of the mountain, striving to take advantage of my distraction, and put some territory between us. I was in no way worried, as he'd slowed considerable, what with the loss of blood and all. I'd've even lingered longer on the top of Mount Tahoma, pixilated as I was on what I saw, but that a blizzard commenced to blow out of nowhere and forced me to decamp for more amiable climes.

HANNAH GYNT: And did you lose him in that blizzard? Is that where it happened?

PEER: No, m'am. I did not lose that buck. Most men would have been discouraged, but I persevered. I tracked him through that raging blizzard, even though I couldn't see my hand in front of my face, or feel my frozen feet. I tracked that buck back down the mountainside, across a dozen glaciers, and finally caught up to him at the edge of a mighty cliff, a sheer precipice, an icy falls, a frozen cataract—

HANNAH GYNT: At last! So now he's in your sight again, trapped and no escape—

PEER: I was up above him on a ledge. I drew a bead, took aim through the pelting snow, and fired!

HANNAH GYNT: Land's sake. And then what happened?

PEER: Exactly nothing.

HANNAH GYNT: Nothing? What on earth d'you mean, nothing?

PEER: I mean nothing, nohow, diddly squat! My powder'd gotten wet and my rifle misfired. The buck turned his head and cocked an ear. He'd somehow heard—don't ask me how—the click of the hammer through the howling storm, and was making ready to bolt. So I hurled my worthless weapon aside, threw myself off the ledge, landed upon the buck's broad-beamed back, and grabbed onto his antlers for dear life. He was so startled—

HANNAH GYNT: And who wouldn't be, I declare, some damn fool jumped on top of you—

PEER: He leapt off the cliff, into thin air, and we sailed a mile into

men's and women's scenes 7

space, falling faster and faster through the heart of the storm. Everything was white, the wind was rushing past, we were flying through the snow! Down! Down! Down! We dropped through the clouds, we scattered eagles, we passed so close to a lightning bolt I could have reached out and grabbed it! In fact, I did! Just plucked it! On impulse, without thinking—and then let go of that durned lightning bolt in a San Francisco second, but not before I'd burned an indelible zigzag scar across the palm of my hand—

(He shows her his palm, which has a zigzag scar across it Hannah gasps.)

HANNAH GYNT: My word! *Peer!*

PEER: A celestial souvenir of my escapade, and proof positive of my veracity. But I had no time to dwell upon the pain and sizzle of my poor mortified flesh! Down we fell, through the heavens, dropping faster and faster! Then the clouds cleared, and below us I could see our reflection in an icy lake, getting bigger and bigger, coning up fast! And then we hit! A mighty splash!

HANNAH GYNT: A mighty rude awakening!

PEER: The buck was so heavy, and we were dropping so fast, we plunged straight to the bottom of that freezing lake. Must've been a mile or more. I held my breath and hung on. Then we swam for the surface. My lungs were bursting! I was out of breath and growing dizzy. The world was turning black, my life swimming before by eyes, I thought of you—

HANNAH GYNT: Did you, Peer? Did you?

PEER: I did Ma, I swear you were my last thought before I went to meet my maker.

HANNAH GYNT: Ah, that's sweet. But then what happened?

PEER: We were under water so long by the time we got back up to the surface a sheet of ice three feet thick had formed across it. The buck butted his head against the ice, once, twice, three times. I could feel him losing strength, giving up hope. I thought we were done for. With the last ounce of gumption I had in me, I jabbed my heels into his flanks, he

8 men's and women's scenes

bucked like a wild bronco, his antlers cracked the ice and split it open, we breached up into the blessed air and splashed ashore.

HANNAH GYNT: Thank heaven a second time, and a third. And then?

PEER: It was so cold and I was so tired and weak from my various travails, my clothes froze solid, my fingers blue, my poor palm sore as blazes from where I grabbed that piece of greasy lightning—

HANNAH GYNT: Yes, son? Yes?

PEER: I lost my grip slipped off the buck, and he got away. Vamoosed, as it were.

HANNAH GYNT: Oh, Peer. You poor boy. What a shame. To come so close and work so hard, and end up with nothing. Ain't that just like life?

PEER: Yup. Ain't it? Ain't it just?

(He nods solemnly, then grins. He can't help revealing his pleasure in putting over his story. She catches his smirk and knows she's been deceived. She swats him, angry.)

HANNAH GYNT: Liar! I swear. This lie just gets bigger and bigger every time you tell it. You ought to be ashamed of yourself. And double shame on me for believing even one word for a single second, Scamp! What about that scar?

PEER: Oh, this? I got this going over a barbed wire fence.

HANNAH GYNT: Besides, now I recollect. You didn't even make that story up, the boy and the buck, you got it out of some book of tall tales or other and embroidered it to suit you. You haven't been out hunting at all, have you? You've been hiding from Smitty. My son, the coward. Ever since he thrashed you within an inch of your scrawny life—

PEER: He ain't thrashed me. 'Case you're curious, I thrashed him.

HANNAH GYNT: Listen to him. Look what I raised. A brawler, a hooligan—

PEER: Ah, Ma, listen to you. Brawler or coward. You're in a tizzy either way. What happened between Smitty and me was less than nothing. He questioned my veracity, is all, and I had to put him in his place.

HANNAH GYNT: Imagine that. Someone questioning *your* veracity. Well, well, well.

PEER: Some folks are plain ignorant Ma. The world's full of 'em.

BAFO (Best and Final Offer)
Tom Strelich

Man & Woman
Shokanje (mid-20's-30's) a former Marine now employed in human resources; an African-American woman straddling two worlds, and P. K. (30's-40's) a disgruntled ex-employee; armed and dangerous.

Scene: the conference room of a small defense contractor in the declining Southern California defense/aerospace industry

> *P.K. has entered the building of his former place of employment armed for bear. When he confronts his former co-workers in a conference room, he and Shokanje are pulled into a deadly debate.*

SHOKANJE: Look, why don't you just call me a nigger and get it over with.
(Clay stands beside the gun, waits for an opening.)
P.K.: Why would I do that?
SHOKANJE: Because that's how you guys always are—sexist, racist...
P.K.: Because I don't like black women's titties? I hardly think that makes me...
SHOKANJE: I met a lot of you in the Marine Corps—a cross-burning, pickup-truck-with-a-Confederate-flag-bumpersticker-driving, lifetime-NRA-Nazi-gun-freak crazy little white boy racist.
P.K.: *(Beat.)* I have unconditional love for you people, always have, ever since you were just colored. You frighten me, mystify me, but I cherish you. I would never use the n-word, I have too much respect for your race. Even if you don't. You

call each other the n-word all de doo-dum day, and think nothing of it.

SHOKANJE: So what? Jews and gays do the same thing, open self-contempt is one of the few perks of oppression and persecution...

(Shokanje sees Clay near the gun.)

P.K.: But call each other "white" or "white-acting" and watch the fur fly...(Struck by a thought, turning to the others.) She knows what ontological means.

SHOKANJE: Yeah. And eschatological too. *(As if to explain.)* Catholic school.

P.K.: Then you've definitely been called white a few times, haven't you? And there's nothing worse than being white.

(P.K. notices Clay near the gun, turns away, smiles to himself.)

SHOKANJE: Oh yeah, it must be really tough being a white man in America. *(Watching Clay.)* Look, why don't you do the world a favor and plug that shotgun in your mouth and make pizza on the wall. That's what you're eventually gonna do anyway. That's what you guys always do. That's *your* eschatology. Shoot everybody, then shoot yourself 'cause you don't want to get in trouble. *(Imitating.)* "Oh shit, I've done it now. Lookit all these dead people." Cut out the middle man, shoot yourself first.

P.K.: Well, thanks for the input. Excellent suggestion, well-reasoned and articulately expressed, but I can't minimize the importance of the middle man in this transaction. So is that it then?

SHOKANJE: Is what it?

P.K.: Your best and final offer? *(Raising the video camera.)* Don't you want to ask for anything? I mean, I've never seen a black open their mouth without axing for something.

SHOKANJE: What, you mean like, freedom, respect, equal opportunity?

P.K.: Yeah, *(Lowering the camera.)* shit like that—dignity, kindness, acceptance, the usual. Like I've got big stockpiles of it or something, that I'm hoarding, keeping to myself. Like I'm in charge. I'm tired of people asking me for shit that I don't have. I don't have it! I can't give it! There's nothing left, there was nothing here! When are people going to get that through their thick skulls! Why does it have to take a bullet! *(She vomits noisily in the trashcan.)*

P.K.: *(Looking on, shaking his head.)* You know what I'm sick of? *(To no one in particular.)* Black women's voices, singing. They're everywhere. *(To Clay.)* Have you noticed? It used to be that that colored, I mean Negro, I mean black, I mean African-American Gospel sound was reserved exclusively for the praise of God, Jesus, and the Heavenly pay-back. Now it praises AT&T long distance, cold-filtered beer, and minivans.

SHOKANJE: Another example of the white corporate power structure looting black, *(Catching herself.)* African-American culture for the bottom line.

P.K.: *(To Shokanje.)* But why can't you just pick a note and sing it for a while? Why do you have to do that gospel shit and flutter all over the place…

SHOKANJE: You mean like Joe Cocker and Michael Bolton and all those other milky-faced Ray Charles wannabe's?…

P.K.: *(Not hearing, continuing the thought.)* Rubbing our noses in how much soul you have. Like the rest of us don't or something. You think only the suffering can feel, only the oppressed have insight, wisdom? Not reedy-voiced, middle-class white men plodding through life? Only whispering shamans, grunting primitives, and croaking black women… fuck Maya Angelou!

SHOKANJE: Don't you talk about Maya that way, don't you even be talking about Maya that way! You don't want to go there. You ain't worthy to drink her bathwater, *(Mocking.)* yunnstan I'm sayn? You ain't worthy to eat the corn outta her shit! You pencil-dicked, monkey-balled, finger-on-the-trigger, finger-on-the-button, finger-on-every-Goddamn-thing snow-flake white-bread muhvuga! All you got is that *(the gun)*. That's all you got. You know that. You can't bring life into this world, so you take it. Take it however you can, assault-rifles, atom bombs, cruise-missiles, submarines, X-ray lasers, nerve gas, particle-beam weapons, death-from-above-Star-Wars-mutual-assured-destruction-endgame scenario-bullshit—there ain't nothing in this world more dangerous than a scared white man!

P.K.: *(Focusing the camera.)* Mega-dittos.

A Body Not Greatly Changed

Jo J. Adamson

Man & Woman

Gale (late 20's) a depressed young woman on the verge of suicide and Dr. Franklin (40's-50's) her shrink.

Scene: a psychiatrist's office

> *Gale's husband has ordered her to seek help from a psychiatrist in an effort to combat what he perceives to be her growing sense of ennui. In reality, Gale can no longer discern meaning in her life. Pregnant and depressed, Gale here pays a visit to Dr. Franklin, knowing that she will never see him again.*

> *Lights U.C. of stage. There is a Ben Franklin, Psychiatrist seated at desk. He's writing something on pad. The intercom buzzes. He picks it up.*

DOCTOR BEN: Yes?, she's here. *(Doctor Ben consults watch.)* Fifteen minutes late. She's improving. Last week it was a half hour. Send her in, June.
(Gale is in shadow area of stage. We hear her voice but see her only in shadow. She pins hair on top of her head and slips into jacket.)
GALE: And you, Doctor Ben are ten years late. There's nothing you can do for me. I'm just killing time.
(Gale moves U.C. Light illuminates her as she comes into view of Doctor Ben. Gale is now 28.)
GALE: Good morning, Doctor Ben.
(Doctor Ben rises.)

DOCTOR BEN: Good morning, Gale. My, you're in a chipper mood.

GALE: Been outside yet? It's gorgeous.

(Ben indicates that Gale sits. She finds a comfortable chair and sits down. She is facing her doctor, however.)

BEN: Yes, I've been out. I went to lunch.

(Gale giggles.)

GALE: My psychiatrist is out to lunch.

(Ben smiles, a bit strained.)

BEN: I've returned.

(Gale smiles.)

GALE: So you have.

BEN: What would you like to talk about today?

GALE: Your name for starters. Benjamin Franklin. I expect you to pull lightning down from the sky or something.

DOCTOR BEN: Actually, Franklin's experiment had to do with verifying the identity of electricity and lightning, Gale.

GALE: Whatever. Did your mother think you were going to "verify" lightning or something. I mean what kind of mother would name her kid after a American icon for Christ's sakes.

(Franklin not too comfortable with the idea himself. He's a bit defensive.)

BEN: She was halfway there with the name Franklin, so she just added the Ben.

(As Doctor Ben says this, he realizes how that must sound to Gale, but it is too late to revise.)

GALE: Added the Ben! My God, you're a fuckin' add on!

DOCTOR BEN: We're going nowhere with this. What do you want to talk about today?

GALE: Actually, nothing. I'd rather be sailing. Why don't *you* pick a topic?

DOCTOR BEN: It'll have to pertain to you.

GALE: Oh Christ, yes.

BEN: I'd like you to tell me about your parents—particularly your mother.

GALE: My mother was very particular. Especially about getting

16 men's and women's scenes

crumbs on the carpet. Or drawing pictures in the steam on the bathroom mirror.

BEN: Yes?

(Gale gets up and goes over to wall. She looks at Ben's credentials.)

GALE: At the risk of boring you, Doctor Ben. I had a shamefully normal childhood. Mother never forgot my birthday and daddy kissed away "the ouches." We went on so many family outings, the mere mention of lemonade makes me run to the nearest picnic table.

(Doctor Ben is ever patient with Gale.)

DOCTOR BEN: You lost your father when you were quite young. Do you want to tell me more about that?

GALE: No. He died. That about covers it.

(Gale returns to the chair. She sits. The two regard one another.)

DOCTOR BEN: Would you like to tell me what has been on your mind during the last week?

GALE: No.

DOCTOR BEN: What are you feeling?, Gale.

GALE: I am nothing, Doctor Ben.

BEN: You're *feeling* nothing.

GALE: I'm not describing a sensation. I'm stating a fact.

BEN: Alright, let's go with that. How did you become nothing?

GALE: It wasn't easy. It took years of hard work.

(Ben looks at his note pad.)

DOCTOR BEN: Last week you told me about a recurring nightmare. A nightmare where you saw a … "mountain of dry ice moving toward you."

GALE: It's getting closer, Doctor.

BEN: You had the dream again?

GALE: Last night. The dry ice mountain is at my doorstep. *(Dryly.)* I've only to bring it in with the Sunday Comics.

BEN: Why do you think you dream of dry ice?

(Gale gets up and moves around room. She stops at table where there is a copper sea gull sculpture.)

GALE: Isn't that something you seed clouds with? To make it rain?

DOCTOR BEN: It's been used for that.

GALE: I guess I'd like to have it rain inside me. I'd like to be able to *cry*. *(Gale picks up the sculpture, turns it over in her hands.)* I want to feel something.

DOCTOR BEN: Be careful Gale. The edges are sharp.

(Gale puts the sculpture down.)

GALE: They'd be better off without me.

DOCTOR BEN: Who?

GALE: All of them. Robert, my mother, Forrest. The life that is growing inside me.

DOCTOR BEN: What are you saying, Gale?

(Gale comes back to the chair. She sits down.)

GALE: Nothing. Say, are you married?

DOCTOR BEN: Not anymore. We mutually agreed to live apart. Why do you ask?

GALE: Just curious. And that's something! I haven't wanted to know anything since I found the blood stain on my panties when I was thirteen.

DOCTOR BEN: Do you feel you've changed in the six months since I've been seeing you?

GALE: I've gotten pregnant. And I promise not to hold you responsible.

DOCTOR BEN: Why are you seeing me, Gale?

GALE: You know that Robert set it up. He insisted that I get professional help. He said I wasn't capable of making the simplest decisions.

DOCTOR BEN: Do you agree with him?

GALE: To live with Robert is to agree with him. Anyway, there's nothing wrong with me that a baby and a Caribbean cruise wouldn't care.

DOCTOR BEN: You mentioned the cruise last week. When are you leaving?

GALE: Friday, next.

DOCTOR BEN: That soon?

18 men's and women's scenes

GALE: I want to look good in a bikini and the meter's running. *(Gale looks closely at Doctor Ben.)* I bought one today. Do you want to see it? *(Without waiting for an answer, Gale reaches into a bag and pulls out an emerald green bikini.)*

DOCTOR BEN: Very nice.

(Gale holds it up to her body.)

DOCTOR BEN: I'm not interested in seeing you in that, Gale.

(Gale puts suit back in package.)

GALE: Suit yourself. Oh, sorry about that.

DOCTOR BEN: Do you want to take this trip?

GALE: What woman wouldn't welcome the opportunity?

DOCTOR BEN: *(Doctor Ben consults his appointment book.)* Two weeks from today then. The fifteenth.

GALE: *(Flat.)* That'll be fine. *(Gale gets up and extends her hand.)* Good-by, Doctor Ben.

(Doctor Ben takes her hand. He finds her behavior curious. She has never taken his hand before upon leaving, but he does not say anything.)

DOCTOR BEN: Until next time, Gale. Send me a postcard from somewhere in the Caribbean.

(Gale pulls her hand from his grasp. She goes to the door and opens it. Gale exits. Doctor Ben notices swimsuit on floor next to the desk. He rushes over to pick it up, and holds the package in front of him. He says redundantly:)

DOCTOR BEN: Gale, wait!...You forgot...

(Lights go down as Doctor Ben holds the swimsuit in his hand.)

The Buffoon Piece

Bob Jude Ferrante

2 Men & 1 Woman

Alessandro (25) an actor in Commedia Dell'Arte; naive and optimistic, Peter (35) a German intellectual who has recently escaped from a labor camp with the aid of Marina (36) a fellow prisoner and intellectual peer.

Scene: a barn in Volpe Nero, Italy. Autumn, 1936

> *Peter and Marina have escaped from their work camp and made their way to Italy, narrowly avoiding capture at every turn. They have taken sanctuary in a barn belonging to Alessandro. As Hitler and Mussolini prepare to formalize the Rome-Berlin Axis, Peter and Marina reveal the unknown horrors of the work camps to their host.*

> *Lights. Barn interior. Straw floor, empty stalls. Peter and Marina, lay in straw, eating from a pot and skin.*

PETER: Marina?
   (Silence.)
MARINA: What?
PETER: It's the life.
MARINA: Any stew left?
PETER: Yeah. The life?
   (Passes her the pot. Enter Alessandro, unseen.)
MARINA: The life.
PETER: Food is *good*!
   (Marina stares at Peter. Silence.)
ALESSANDRO: Hello!
MARINA: *(Startled, drops the pot.)* Oh!

20 men's and women's scenes

ALESSANDRO: Don't worry. I'm a friend (Pause.) Sorry about your lunch… Do you like my barn?

MARINA: Your barn? It is…lovely.

PETER: The straw is warm.

ALESSANDRO: It clean?

MARINA: Mostly, yes.

(Beat.)

ALESSANDRO: Are the Blackshirts looking for you?

PETER: The Blackshirts?!

ALESSANDRO: Don't worry. We sold our last pig—no animals. Just this building. You're safe.

MARINA: You would not get in trouble?

ALESSANDRO: It's *our* barn. I'm Alessandro.

MARINA: I am called Marina. He is —

PETER: I want to say it! *(Pause.)* Peter. My name is Peter.

ALESSANDRO: Marina… Pietro?

MARINA: That is right.

ALESSANDRO: Great! Where's your home?

PETER: Gone!

MARINA: We are German. From Gernsbach.

(Awkward pause.)

ALESSANDRO: The Germans killed my brother.

(Beat. Marina jumps up.)

MARINA: Up, Peter. We have to leave now.

(Peter jumps up.)

ALESSANDRO: Wait! I'm not going to…you thought I would—?

MARINA: Wouldn't you?

ALESSANDRO: No.

(Beat.)

MARINA: I am sorry about your brother.

ALESSANDRO: So am I. *(Pause.)* He was kind of a pain in the ass. *(Pause.)* I mean, I still *miss* him…

(Beat.)

MARINA: (Softer.) What do you do?

ALESSANDRO: Huh? Actor.

PETER: My trade is journalist.

ALESSANDRO: What happened?

PETER: I write *one* anti-Nazi article. Bang! To camp with him!

ALESSANDRO: Camp?

MARINA: For *politicals*—ha! I am a graduate student. *(Pause.)* Did Mussolini sign the agreement with Hitler?

ALESSANDRO: Radio said he was in Berlin yesterday.

MARINA: I fear there will be an alliance. You know what those are for? A war.

ALESSANDRO: When?

MARINA: Soon.

ALESSANDRO: Another war! We just *had* one.

MARINA: I am sorry.

(Pause.)

ALESSANDRO: You hungry?

MARINA: We just ate. Thanks. Stew was great. The boy...said it was...your mother's?

ALESSANDRO: No. Mother's dead. I do the cooking. And my wife.

MARINA: You are married?

ALESSANDRO: Yeah. Why?

MARINA: You look too young... Anyway, your stew was good.

ALESSANDRO: Thanks. But I didn't make it. My cousin's mother.

MARINA: Oh, *Culo*?

ALESSANDRO: *Ciulio. Culo* is 'asshole!'

MARINA: My Italian is not perfect. *(Alessandro sits.)* Would you like to see something? Between friends?

ALESSANDRO: Friends. Sure.

(Peter looks on, confused.)

MARINA: In a way, a fashion thing. Maybe it becomes popular.

PETER: *(Reaches to stop her.) Es ist verboten, deine Nummer zu shauen.*

MARINA: Somebody must tell *somebody*.

ALESSANDRO: What's this all about?

PETER: *Verboten.*

MARINA: Look. *(Rolls up her sleeve.)*

ALESSANDRO: You hurt?

MARINA: Here.

22 men's and women's scenes

ALESSANDRO: A number. Fashion thing, you said? What's it for?

PETER: What's it...!

MARINA: For nothing, any more.

ALESSANDRO: Then why show it?

MARINA: It is my *name*.

ALESSANDRO: Your name is Marina.

MARINA: What a sweet boy. *This* is my name.

ALESSANDRO: Name.

PETER: Millions of Marinas... Peters... These names are common. But to each, only one number. *(Shows Alessandro his number.)* Race. Religion. Sexual preference. Crime. Encoded.

ALESSANDRO: Name. *(Touches Marina's arm gently. Rubs the number.)*

MARINA: It is under my skin. Does not come off. The *kapos* call you by number.

ALESSANDRO: You have *Capos*? Do they run your market?

MARINA: No, they are prisoners like us. The SS lets them run the camp.

ALESSANDRO: Call you by number! Numbers are for prices. Sums.

MARINA: Names. Paul. I loved him! I'd never shoot him. But what about R-332689? Easier. 'X' it out. Ink spills, hands stay clean. Memorize your number. Stare at the fence. Wait.

ALESSANDRO: For what?

MARINA: To die.

PETER: Escape. Eat. Breathe. Run!

MARINA: Die.

PETER: Yes. Die.

(Pause.)

MARINA: Sometimes we ate gruel. Made of, I think, grass, vegetables. Then a friend would disappear. Next day...in your bowl...

PETER: *(Whispers.) Verboten.*

MARINA: You would have a slice of meat. You would eat it. You would not ask the source. You wait to be saved.

PETER: Die.

MARINA: Yes.

ALESSANDRO: Numbers, grass. No hope?

MARINA: You *are* young. Learn, sweet boy. Because you can die fighting, run, fake it, survive. Or there is…
(Silence.)

ALESSANDRO: Not that I felt good before, but now…

PETER: He learns.

MARINA: Bound to catch up with you sometime.
(Darkness.)

Cute Lonely Guys Looking for You

John Attanas

Man & Woman
Keith (30) a social worker and Stephanie (20's) his girlfriend; a model.

Scene: NYC

> *Here a comically mismatched couple enjoys a less-than-satis-factory evening at home.*

O   O   O

STEPHANIE: Do you really like me with short hair?
  (Beat.)
KEITH: What?
STEPHANIE: I could cut it.
KEITH: Your hair's fine.
STEPHANIE: But in the picture.
KEITH: What picture?
STEPHANIE: The one I showed you.
  (Keith thinks. Beat. Then remembers.)
KEITH: Oh.
STEPHANIE: You told me you liked the way I looked with short hair.
KEITH: I like the way you look all the time.
STEPHANIE: Even with long hair?
KEITH: Especially with long hair.
  (Keith goes back to his reading. Short pause.)
STEPHANIE: What are you reading?
KEITH: The *Times*.
STEPHANIE: I know that. What are you reading in the *Times*?
KEITH: Hungary's having economic problems.

STEPHANIE: Why?

KEITH: Converting from a command economy to a market economy isn't easy.

(Stephanie looks at the newspaper and freezes.)

STEPHANIE: Oh, God.

KEITH: What?

STEPHANIE: Celeste Mattei. For Bergdorf's. Everywhere I look, she's there. She was supposed to show up last night. I wish we hadn't left so early.

KEITH: The music was so loud…

STEPHANIE: And her hair is so short. Short hair is coming back. Even you like short hair.

KEITH: I do not like short hair.

STEPHANIE: You said you did.

KEITH: In one picture. Now relax. And let me finish the article. Okay?

STEPHANIE: I'm sorry, honey.

KEITH: *(To the audience.)* She let me read for exactly thirty seconds, then…

STEPHANIE: Let's play a game.

KEITH: What?

STEPHANIE: I know a great game we haven't played.

KEITH: Honey…

STEPHANIE: I say a word. And you've got to say a word that begins with the last letter of the word I said. And then I have to do the same. You only get ten seconds, and if you repeat a word, you lose. And no names, only words.

KEITH: Honey…

STEPHANIE: Pleeeaaassseee.

(Beat.)

KEITH: You start.

(She thinks.)

STEPHANIE: Yak.

KEITH: King.

(Quick beat.)

STEPHANIE: Gorilla.

26 men's and women's scenes

KEITH: Albatross.

STEPHANIE: S..? Sol.

KEITH: That's a name.

STEPHANIE: Sol?

KEITH: It's a Jewish name.

STEPHANIE: It's Spanish for sun.

KEITH: You're allowed to use Spanish words?

STEPHANIE: Sure.

KEITH: You didn't say that.

STEPHANIE: I didn't say you couldn't. Let's start again.

KEITH: We can use Spanish words?

STEPHANIE: Any words.

KEITH: How about Icelandic?

STEPHANIE: (Annoyed.) Keith.

KEITH: Okay. You start.

> *(Beat.)*

STEPHANIE: Yak.

KEITH: King.

STEPHANIE: Gorilla.

KEITH: Albatross.

> *(Quick beat.)*

STEPHANIE: Sleep.

KEITH: Pipe.

STEPHANIE: Elevator.

KEITH: Room.

> *(Quick beat.)*

STEPHANIE: Mattress.

KEITH: Screen.

STEPHANIE: Normal.

KEITH: Line

> *(Quick beat.)*

STEPHANIE: Everett.

KEITH: That's a name.

STEPHANIE: No, it's not.

KEITH: It's a man's name.

STEPHANIE: It's a place. Everett, Washington. My Aunt Sally and
    Uncle Charley live there.
KEITH: It's still a name.
STEPHANIE: It's a place name.
KEITH: You said no names.
STEPHANIE: No *names*. Not no place names.
KEITH: A name is a name. You can't separate place names from
    person's names. They still name something.
    (Quick beat.)
STEPHANIE: What is your problem?
KEITH: What are you talking about?
STEPHANIE: Five minutes ago you didn't even know the game,
    and now you're telling me the rules.
KEITH: Honey…
STEPHANIE: You're no fun at all. You don't even like my hair.
KEITH: I love your hair.
STEPHANIE: Why don't you say so?
KEITH: I just did.
STEPHANIE: Celeste Mattei is getting all the good bookings, and
    you won't even give me emotional support. I'm going to cut
    my hair off at the root!

Epic Poetry

James Bosley

Man & Woman

Pluto (20-40) Sexy and savvy ruler of the underworld and Lief (15)
a young girl searching for her father.

Scene: a mythical time in the New York tri-state area, specifically
the underworld.

> *Lief's search for her lost father, Ulysses, has ended in her
> tragically premature death. Here, she enters the underworld
> and encounters Pluto, who seems to take quite a shine to her
> as she does her best to convince the dark lord to allow her to
> return to earth.*

○ ○ ○

(From the blackness— a voice.)
VOICE: Did you say you never had sex?
LIEF: Who's that?
VOICE: Did you say you never had sex?
LIEF: Yes. Who wants to know?
VOICE: How old are you?
LIEF: Fifteen.
VOICE: And you never?
LIEF: No.
VOICE: Why?
LIEF: I guess because most of the guys I know are geeks.
PLUTO: Greeks?
LIEF: Geeks. Is this a test?
VOICE: It could be. Wait right there.
    (Lief waits. Pluto enters. He's a sexy guy.)
LIEF: Are you God?
PLUTO: I'm a god. Pluto some call me. Not to be confused with

the Disney dog. Master of the Underworld. I don't get many virgins down here these days. Will you marry me?

LIEF: I beg you pardon?

PLUTO: Will you marry me?

LIEF: Gee, I don't know. It's a little sudden.

PLUTO: It's not like you have a lot of choice you know. It's me or no one at all. Forever.

LIEF: Can I think about it?

PLUTO: I'm very good in bed.

LIEF: Yeah but, I mean, I've had a really trying day.

PLUTO: You see, every so often, when the world is a mess—dirty, violent, petty—like it is now, and people have no hope, the future looks bleak, they don't believe in gods, that's when I take it upon myself to make a virgin my bride. You're a very pretty girl.

LIEF: So, you marry a virgin and—what? She gives birth to a redeemer? Restores purity to the world? Something like that?

PLUTO: No. I marry a virgin because it cheers me up. But if you marry me you get to be my Queen. You get a throne, very nice, very comfy. You get a crown bejeweled with the fine stones. You get all sorts of special privileged. And best of all you get me.

LIEF: Do I get to return to the land of the living?

PLUTO: Who do you think you are, Jesus Christ? Damn, everyone wants to return to the living. It used to be when people came here they knew there was no return ticket. Then I made an exception—Gilgamesh. Nice kid. Came looking for his dead friend. Gay I think, whatever. I took pity and it's like I opened up the floodgates. Psyche. Orpheus. Hercules comes, steals my dog, and frees the soul of Theseus! I get Dante. I get Aeneas. I get Lazarus. I get Tinkerbell! People started thinking they could come and go as they pleased. What am I running here? A Stop'n Shop? The final straw, I get this guy, wants to talk to the spirit of blind Teiresias. He's got connections in high places so I say okay. Next thing I know they're having a party! He's talking to his mother, he's talking to his Trojan War buddies...soon all the souls are worked up and howling like banshees. And I hate when that happens. You ever hear a room full of souls all howling at once?

LIEF: No.

PLUTO: It's awful.

LIEF: What was his name?

PLUTO: Odysseus.

LIEF: Odysseus?

PLUTO: The man mocks me. Mocks me! I had him on the threshold dozens of times—swallowed by boiling seas, his body a squirming morsel in the jaws of ravenous monsters, his blood a gushing fountain on the fields of Troy. And each time he escaped. And after each escape he laughed at me. He enjoys it! Brags about it! It's blasphemous! And then he has the beans to waltz into my domain, stir up my dead, and waltz out, like he's the fucking tooth fairy! But he can't beat me forever. No mortal can.

LIEF: He's my father.

PLUTO: You're pulling my leg.

LIEF: Odysseus. From Ithaca. But we call him Otis.

PLUTO: That's him.

LIEF: When was he here?

PLUTO: When? We don't have "whens" down here. We don't have Time. So, Odysseus was your father, ay?

LIEF: I was searching for him when—when I died.

PLUTO: That's very interesting. Tell me, how did you die, such a young girl.

LIEF: I was crossing a bridge when it collapsed, but I don't think it was accidental. There was an old woman, she put a curse on me.

PLUTO: A cantankerous old woman? With a bag of tricks? Disguises, potions and what not?

LIEF: Yes.

PLUTO: Calliope.

LIEF: Calliope? The goddess of epic poetry?

PLUTO: Hey I'm impressed, you know your gods and goddesses. Technically she's only a muse but try telling her that, pompous old biddy. So she put a curse on you. And you're the virgin daughter of Odysseus. Very interesante. It sounds to me like Destiny is at work here. I think we were meant for each other.

LIEF: But if that's true, I'd have to complete my quest first— Return to the living, find my father. Otherwise destiny won't be satisfied.

PLUTO: Weisenheimer.

LIEF: Can't you make one more exception?

PLUTO: Under the circumstances—

LIEF: I promise to come back.

PLUTO: You don't have to promise. I'll come get you.

LIEF: Could you help me find him?

PLUTO: I don't think that's exactly kosher. Who knows what Calliope has planned. But I will put you on the right path because I don't want you wandering around up there for years getting old. I like you the way you are.

LIEF: Does that mean I can go?

PLUTO: I'm thinking about it.

LIEF: I promise to remain a virgin.

PLUTO: No.

LIEF: No?

PLUTO: No. Sex first.

LIEF: Sex? First?

PLUTO: That's the deal.

LIEF: But then I won't be a virgin.

PLUTO: No fooling.

LIEF: But will you still want me?

Pluto; You mean will I respect you in the morning? Don't worry, my word is truth. Death and taxes, right?

LIEF: But—

PLUTO: Suddenly I want you very badly.

LIEF: You do?

PLUTO: Yes, virgin daughter of Odysseus. Yes.

32 men's and women's scenes

LIEF: Right now?

PLUTO: I think the time is right.

LIEF: But—

PLUTO: Scared?

LIEF: Uh-huh.

PLUTO: That's normal.

LIEF: This is not the way I thought it would happen.

PLUTO: It never is. Ask anybody.

LIEF: I know but—

PLUTO: What do you want, music? Soft lights?

> *(Suddenly the lights change to a romantic hue. Frank Sinatra sings "Nice n Easy.")*

PLUTO: You like Frankie?

LIEF: I guess.

> *(He holds out his pinky.)*

PLUTO: So we have a deal or what?

> *(Lief hesitates.)*

PLUTO: Face it, you don't have much to lose.

> *(Lief holds up her pinky. They move toward each other, pinkies out to seal the bargain.)*

PLUTO: Fear not. It will be—divine.

> *(Their pinkies touch. Ecstasy overcomes them both. There is a flash of white light.)*

The Exception

Olga Humphrey

Man & Woman
Artemisia Gentileschi (18) a talented and tempestuous artist and
Fabrizio Ursino (50's) a patron of the arts with suspect motives.

Scene: Rome 1611

> *Artemisia is determined to make her mark as a great painter
> despite the fact of her gender. Here, the driven young
> woman is forced to swallow her pride in order to cultivate
> new patrons.*

O   O   O

> *Artemisia's studio. Gone is the order that Orazio brought to
> his work space. Artemisia's is filled with canvases, paints,
> brushes, etc., a glorious, colorful mayhem. Artemisia is with
> a client: Fabrizio Ursino, a well-dressed and milquetoast-look-
> ing man in his fifties. She is showing him a painting.*

ARTEMISIA: The paint's not quite dry, but I wanted you to see it.
  What do you think?

FABRIZIO: Signorina Gentileschi, it is simply and undeniably
  exquisite.

ARTEMISIA: I'm so happy you like it. This was such a specific commission that I felt a great deal of pressure in executing it to
  your satisfaction.

FABRIZIO: I am very, very satisfied, Signorina Gentileschi. God
  guides your paintbrush. I must get down on my knees this
  moment… *(He falls to his knees before the canvas.)*

ARTEMISIA: Signor Ursino, that's really not necessary.

FABRIZIO: No, I must. I am, before you, and these beautiful four
  naked women that you have painted for me, most humble.

ARTEMISIA: You are most kind. *(She helps him back to his feet.)*
FABRIZIO: May I ask about how you work? I am simply fascinated, you see. The process. Tell me of the process.
ARTEMISIA: Certainly. I usually begin by determining how much canvas I will need for the execution of the work. I stretch my own rather than have one of my father's assistants do so...
FABRIZIO: No, I meant the four naked women.
ARTEMISIA: Of course, they are not simply women. They are allegories...
FABRIZIO: Such perfectly proportioned allegories. You do use live models, do you not?
ARTEMISIA: Yes, of course.
FABRIZIO: And they do pose in this disrobed state, do they not?
ARTEMISIA: As you see in the painting.
FABRIZIO: It's so fascinating to think of a beautiful young woman such as yourself gazing upon the nakedness of four other women with such intensity as must be required for the execution of your craft.
ARTEMISIA: I discern that you are a true art lover, Signor Ursino. *(Beat.)* I must ask for the payment.
FABRIZIO: Oh, yes, yes. *(He pulls coins from his pocket.)* Fifty ducats as promised. And here is an extra ten ducats in appreciation of your talent.
ARTEMISIA: Thank you so much.
FABRIZIO: There should be more women artists like you.
ARTEMISIA: Painting naked women, of course.
FABRIZIO: You see my point. *(Beat.)* May I ask what is the most difficult aspect of your work?
ARTEMISIA: For me, it's usually the composition, but perhaps "difficult" isn't quite the right word. It's the most "challenging" aspect, I would say, because it requires a certain amount of preparation and planning before one can even set paint to canvas.
FABRIZIO: Oh, yes, yes. And do you find the human body itself more difficult to execute than physical objects?
ARTEMISIA: No, not at all. .

men's and women's scenes 35

FABRIZIO: Not even the...uhhhhh...uhhhhh... *(He points to the canvas.)*

ARTEMISIA: Breasts?

FABRIZIO: More specifically the...uhhhhh...uhhhh...

ARTEMISIA: Nipples, signor?

FABRIZIO: Oh, yes, yes.

(Artemisia is on to Fabrizio.)

ARTEMISIA: No, but the fleshy buttocks, so like a plucked sun-ripened Neapolitan peach, can be exacting.

FABRIZIO: *(Overwhelmed.)* Signorina Gentileschi, in further appreciation of your brilliance, I would like to commission another work by you.

ARTEMISIA: I have an idea.

FABRIZIO: Oh, please, tell me.

ARTEMISIA: I suggest a painting of—

FABRIZIO: Oh, yes, yes!

ARTEMISIA: *Five* naked women!

FABRIZIO: I am speechless, Signorina Gentileschi. Not a peep. Not half a peep can express—

ARTEMISIA: We are agreed then.

FABRIZIO: Signorina Gentileschi. I am willing to pay you double your price if you would paint the five naked women while you are also unclothed. And I would be honored to be present as a witness to your creative genius.

ARTEMISIA: And will you yourself be nude?

FABRIZIO: Oh, no. I am not at all artistic.

ARTEMISIA: But you are a dirty old man, aren't you, Signor Ursino?

FABRIZIO: I beg your pardon, Signorina Gentileschi.

ARTEMISIA: You're taking advantage of my sex, aren't you, Signor Ursino?

FABRIZIO: I mean no harm.

ARTEMISIA: I resent you using me in this way for your perverted intentions. Here's your money. You shall not have this painting. *(She takes the canvas away from him.)* I shall be reporting your behavior to my father.

36 men's and women's scenes

FABRIZIO: Oh, please, Signorina Gentileschi. I am sorry. Please do not be angry with me. Please do not take the painting away. I do think it exquisite. Truly, I appreciate your talent. Forgive me my weakness. I am only human and thus frail in so many ways. Aren't we all when it comes to such matters?
(Silence. He panics even more.)
FABRIZIO: Let me make it up to you in some way,
ARTEMISIA: How can you make up for such behavior to me, you...you...what did you say your profession was?
FABRIZIO: A banker.
ARTEMISIA: With what type of clients?
FABRIZIO: Many wealthy clients.
ARTEMISIA: Who, let me guess, commission works of art?
FABRIZIO: Yes?
ARTEMISIA: Nothing comes to you?
FABRIZIO: No.
ARTEMISIA: *(Pointedly.)* We were talking about how you can make up for your behavior as a dirty old banker with many wealthy clients who commission works of art.
(It still takes him a while to get it. Suddenly—)
FABRIZIO: Oh! That's it ! That's it! I shall recommend you to every-one in Rome who passes my way, Signorina Gentileschi. Every client, every patron, every merchant who consults me. I shall tell them, you must, you absolutely must commission a work of art from Signorina Artemisia Gentileschi.
ARTEMISIA: How brilliant of you to come up with this idea all by yourself. Thank you. And I certainly hope that they will not be dirty old men such as yourself.
FABRIZIO: I'm sure not all of them. A few here and there. It goes without saying.
(Artemisia returns the painting.)
FABRIZIO: Thank you, Signorina Gentileschi. Thank you. You shall have so many commissions you will not have a moment's rest.
ARTEMISIA: You do realize I am forced to raise my fee for the new painting.

FABRIZIO: Charge me what you wish. How can one put a price on genius?

ARTEMISIA: I shall start work upon the commission immediately. Five Naked Women Appreciated From Afar by a...God.

FABRIZIO: Oh, yes, yes!

ARTEMISIA: Would you be that God, Signor Ursino? Sit for me.

FABRIZIO: Oh, yes, yes!

ARTEMISIA: Be here tomorrow at the same hour. But, tonight, try, try to get a good night's rest. *(A croak comes out of Fabrizio. She pats him on the back.)* I know. For art, we make the greatest of sacrifices. Until tomorrow, you magnificent God!

Fast Forward

Elyse Nass

Man & Woman

Jeremy (41) a down-on-his-luck novelist and Doris (25) an enthusiastic young woman from Wyoming.

Scene: NYC

Sixteen years after a promising literary debut, Jeremy has lost everything with the exception of his apartment in lower Manhattan where he has been working on the novel he hopes will restore his fame and fortune. Here, the beleaguered writer's home is invaded by Doris, a tornado of a gal who once took his writing seminar and has traveled all the way from Wyoming to pay a most unexpected visit.

O   O   O

At Rise: The place looks exactly the same, except that Doris is in it, making faces at the surroundings. She does a double-take at the clothesline. She holds her ears at the radio that is playing loudly. Doris is attractive, vivacious, dressed in a colorful outfit. Her lightweight coat is draped over a chair. She hears footsteps and takes her coat and clutches it to her. Jeremy enters with bag of Chinese food, sees Doris, is stunned.

JEREMY: Who are you? You're not the woman from the other side of the door?

DORIS: I am the woman from the other side of the door...You left your radio on.

JEREMY: *(Shutting radio off.)* What are you doing here? How'd you get in here?

DORIS: Take it easy. I'm Doris Keegan. Earlier, I buzzed you.

JEREMY: But I didn't buzz you back. I mean, I didn't buzz you in. I didn't let you in.

DORIS: We spoke by the door.

JEREMY: We spoke through the door. But then you went away.

DORIS: Yes…and then I waited outside the building till you left.

JEREMY: What?

DORIS: I thought you'd never leave.

JEREMY: I had to get something to eat. Wait a minute! Why am I telling you this? What are you doing here?

DORIS: I had to see you.

JEREMY: How'd you get in?

DORIS: The woman on the ground floor. I guess she's the landlady. I told her that I was a rare book dealer from Wyoming… and that you had some books for me…And I had a plane to catch…And couldn't she please let me in?

JEREMY: I don't believe this.

DORIS: And she believed me. And let me in. And I looked around and said I couldn't find the rare books. I said you must have them in a special place and would have to wait until you returned. And she stayed with me a few minutes and than said she had to get back to her sick plant Horace. She believed my story. I showed her my student I.D. from Wyoming. But she thought I was a bookdealer.

JEREMY: That's because she can't read.

DORIS: What a shame. I thought there was something wrong.

JEREMY: Doris, I may call the police.

DORIS: Remember, you told me that you don't have a phone.

JEREMY: I make calls from the pay phone downstairs. Wait a minute. Why am I telling you this? You could be some…

DORIS: I'm not a crazy. Don't you remember me? It was one year ago I was in your writing seminar. We even had a small conference…for about an hour. You discussed my work and suggested that I keep a journal. I've followed your advice. I have it here. *(Puts coat back on chair; takes out journal from bag.)* I carry it with me wherever I go. You said, "If you have a thought, jot it down…" Anyway, remember I told you that I worked in a department store in a mall, after I finished high school. It was only recently that I decided to go to college. So I rearranged my hours at the department store around my college schedule...This is my second year, two more to go...And I told you I always had the burning desire to write and signed up for the course...

JEREMY: Yes.

DORIS: I knew you would remember me. I hope you're not angry at me, for coming here so unexpectedly. But it's something I had to do. I know this is your workspace, but it is a bit of a mess...But what kind of place is it?

JEREMY: This is just my workspace.

DORIS: *(Pointing to pages on clothesline.)* What's that?

JEREMY: It's my three different endings for my novel. I hung them up.

DORIS: Gee, that's imaginative.

JEREMY: I haven't decided which ending to go with. I really like looking at all of them...It's like confronting them...

DORIS: Oh, definitely.

JEREMY: There they are...every minute.

DORIS: I know what you mean. *(Pause.)*

JEREMY: Do you know what time it is?

DORIS: *(Looking at her watch.)* Yes. It's twelve P.M. New York time. I changed it when I got here...You don't have a clock here?

JEREMY: No clocks here. Writers hate to watch clocks. I don't even own a watch.

DORIS: That would drive me crazy. How do you know the time?

JEREMY: *(Points to radio.)* The radio. When I need to know, I turn it on...The time comes on...In a matter of minutes...seconds...The radio is a real break for me...In between my work, I listen to music...news, talk radio...breaks the day up...sometimes the evening...if I stay late here...breaks up time...my writing...even write and listen to it...

DORIS: No TV here?

JEREMY: That would be too distracting to have in my workspace.

DORIS: *(Looking around.)* But you have a bed here.

JEREMY: For long naps between writing. Before writing, after writing.

DORIS: And a small kitchen…and bathroom…

JEREMY: Actually, I should tell you that this place once was my apartment.

DORIS: Your apartment?

JEREMY: Yes, many years ago…before my first novel…

DORIS: Before your success.

JEREMY: Yes. *(Pause.)* When I was a struggling writer…After my success, I decided to hold on to it. Use it as a workspace… Nice and quiet in the back. It has no view…just bars on the window…reality of being in a big city. But it's a good neighborhood and the rent is cheap…

DORIS: But you only work here?

JEREMY: Yes. But why am I telling you all this?

DORIS: Is there any chance that I could take, just a peek at you apartment with a skyline?

JEREMY: Well…

DORIS: Imagine seeing a successful writer's apartment. Are you on Fifth Avenue or facing Central Park?

JEREMY: Both.

DORIS: Imagine that. I promise I will not tell one soul where it is. I will protect your privacy totally.

JEREMY: *(Sits down, closes his eyes.)* Light. Give me light.

DORIS: What are you doing?

JEREMY: Meditating. I'm trying to visualize a white light. Once I do, I'll feel better, peaceful.

DORIS: Is that what people are into in New York?

JEREMY: Everybody has some kind of mantra.

DORIS: I think I read about that. (Pause; referring to bag.) Is there food in there?

JEREMY: Oh…I forgot.

DORIS: Whatever it is, I bet it's cold.

JEREMY: It's hard to get that white light right now. *(Gets up; takes out soup and egg roll; begins eating.)* It's a little cold.

DORIS: Do you always eat Chinese food so early in the day?

42 men's and women's scenes

JEREMY: It varies.

DORIS: When you take a break from your work, you go out and get a snack?

JEREMY: Look, Doris. Is this some sort of joke? Or game? Going through all this trouble, telling the landlady a lie...waiting outside for me...Are you some kind of groupie?

DORIS: I had to see you.

JEREMY: Now you've seen me.

DORIS: Yes.

JEREMY: I'm going to have to ask you to—

DORIS: Greetings from the State of Wyoming. *(Takes out some postcards.)* I brought you some postcards.

JEREMY: For me?

DORIS: Yes.

JEREMY: *(Looking at them.)* Wide open...peaceful...beautiful.

DORIS: Here's one with buffaloes grazing. You know, they're very scarce now.

JEREMY: I can imagine.

DORIS: And here's a picture of the meadowlark, the state bird.

JEREMY: You brought these for me?

DORIS: Yes, especially for you...all the way from Wyoming.

JEREMY: That's very nice of you.

DORIS: You're welcome.

JEREMY: I remember what scenic country that was...and the friendliness there...Everybody saying, "Howdy." Wearing jeans and baseball caps...

DORIS: Oh, we're warm, casual people, Mr. Wright. Can I call you Jeremy?

JEREMY: Please do.

DORIS: Jeremy. May I sit down?

JEREMY: I hope this doesn't sound rude...but this is not a very good time for me...not right now. First of all, this place is quite messy...

DORIS: I understand...It's your workspace.

JEREMY: I was working when you came here.

DORIS: So...you haven't finished your novel yet.

JEREMY: Not yet.

DORIS: It sounded like you had almost finished it last year.

JEREMY: I keep rewriting the end...reworking the ending...
changing the ending...*(Pointing to clothesline.)* Those are the
three different endings...in different colors...

DORIS: Yes...So you're working on finishing one of those endings
now...

JEREMY: Well, actually...Why am I telling you all this?

DORIS: Do you always wear jeans and a tee-shirt when you write?

JEREMY: Most of the time.

DORIS: Well, you look so impressive.

JEREMY: Thank you. Do you really think so?

DORIS: Absolutely. You should consider being in ads...I see a lot
of famous people in the arts, posing in magazines...advertis-
ing different products...Why not you?

JEREMY: I don't know.

DORIS: When your book comes out...

JEREMY: Sure. *(Pause.)* You said you were in New York on business? What kind of business?

DORIS: For the store. It's a survey for the store. Meetings with a
few people. Salespeople don't only sell. We do surveys.

JEREMY: I see. *(Pause.)* How long are you here?

DORIS: Ten days.

JEREMY: Then we can meet during the week. I'll feel more
relaxed. We'll do lunch.

DORIS: You're just saying that.

JEREMY: No, I mean it.

DORIS: "Let's do lunch," is a New York expression. I read about
it. Saying it really doesn't mean it. It's just something to say.

JEREMY: But I mean it. I'll call you at your hotel. Where are you
staying?

DORIS: The Bushwick. *(Pause.)* Look, can't you take just a small
break for now? I don't know about lunch. My time is limited
this week. It's not that I'm from the neighborhood. I'm from
Wyoming and here now.
(Pause.)

44 men's and women's scenes

JEREMY: Yes, I know. But you can't seem to take no for an answer. I told you I'm busy and you're still insisting.

DORIS: You sound like I'm rude or something...or a pest.

JEREMY: Well...

DORIS: Is that what you think of me?

JEREMY: Well...You're a nice person...Bringing me postcards... saying nice things about me...You're a real boost to my ego.

DORIS: It wasn't flattery. I was being sincere.

JEREMY: I want to thank you for all that. But I still didn't change my mind.

DORIS: I'm a visitor here.

JEREMY: But I wasn't expecting you.

DORIS: You're rude.

JEREMY: I'm rude?

DORIS: Yes.

JEREMY: You come here unannounced. I told you I couldn't let you in. What did you do? Told some story to the landlady to gain entry...

DORIS: Gain entry? You make me sound like some kind of criminal...

JEREMY: Well it can be considered sort of criminal...

DORIS: I'm not a criminal and you know it.

JEREMY: You invaded my privacy. You had no right to do that.

DORIS: I told you I had to see you.

JEREMY: Why?

DORIS: Well...

JEREMY: Why was it so important to see me?

DORIS: I—not right now. *(Pause.)* You're just rude and not very hospitable. All this time, we've been talking...you haven't offered me a chair...asked me to sit down...I've tried to be pleasant...And now you're accusing me of illegal entry... invasion of privacy...

JEREMY: It's all true...

DORIS: I've tried to be pleasant...But it doesn't matter to you. You don't budge an inch...And you're very insulting...You know something, I don't want to take any more risk...

men's and women's scenes 45

JEREMY: Huh?

(*Doris grabs her coat in a huff, and in her anger, forgets her journal which is on the chair. She rushes out. He sees the journal, picks it up, starts towards door to catch her, and then has a second thought. He sits down and begins to read it.*)
(*Blackout.*)

Fly Me to the Moon

Jocelyn Beard

3 Men & 1 Woman

John Vittorio (30's) and Valya Kormondov (30's), film industry executives and Franco (50's) and Umberto (50's) managers of a small exclusive penzione in the heart of Rome.

Scene: the penzione Agrippi, Rome

> *John and Valya are powerful film producers who have traveled to Rome from Hollywood and Ukraine, respectively, to campaign for their individual films to be included in a Vatican time capsule that will celebrate the new millennium. Although they have never actually met, their movies have been in fierce competition for two years and each is quite scornful of the other's work. Here, they attempt to check into the same hotel with disastrous results.*

O O O

> *John and Valya enter from opposite sides. Both carry luggage and are irritable and exhausted. John Is speaking into his cell phone.*

JOHN: Yeah, yeah, I made it. Look, I can't talk now, Leo. I'm in with a fascinating redheaded signorina who's cooking me angel hair pomodoro as we speak. Catch you later.
(Franco, the manager has appeared.)
FRANCO: May I help…
JOHN: Yes!
VALYA: Yes!
FRANCO: Ahhh, the honeymoon couple from Chicago! Umberto!
JOHN: *(Eyeing Valya.)* Oh, for the love of God. Only me, this could only happen to me.

VALYA: *(Eyeing John.) You*, here? Impossible.

JOHN: I should have known that Sergi would send you to hawk the sword…

FRANCO: Ah, the signora has a sword? I will send someone to fetch it right away! Umberto!

VALYA: I thought you were in Hong Kong.

JOHN: I was.

FRANCO: Escuzi, signore, signora. *(Really hollering.)* UMBERTO!!!

VALYA: Why didn't you stay there?

JOHN: Listen: I've been crammed inside a flying tin can for the last three fucking days of my life and I'm not in the mood.

FRANCO: Ah, signore, once you see our honeymoon suite you will find yourself *(Singing.)* in the mood.

VALYA: Why don't you cram yourself right back inside that tin can and go on back to Hollywood? You have no place here.

JOHN: I have no place here? You, the purveyor of the most anti-God film in the history of anti-God films tell me that I have no place here???

FRANCO: Have no fear! Your room is reserved! Umberto!!!

(As John and Valya continue to escalate their hostilities, Franco continues to attempt pleasant interjections while calling for Umberto.)

VALYA: Anti-God?!?

JOHN: That's right. That's what I said. There's no way that piece of shit is going in the capsule.

VALYA: Piece of shit?!?

JOHN: Are you hearing impaired as well as the century's biggest con-artist?

VALYA: What is this person?

JOHN: Flim flam man!

VALYA: Flim flam? You are calling me this?

JOHN: You bet, lady.

VALYA: But I am not knowing what it is meaning!

JOHN: It means that "The Sword or Redemption" is a four hour long piece of dog doo that you managed to convince the non-thinking minds of this earth is a movie. Now that I finally

48 men's and women's scenes

have a chance to see you...in the flesh...I have an idea of how you were able to hoodwink every distributor at every market.

VALYA: Hoodwink??

JOHN: Well, that ain't gonna work with these boys at the Vatican, sister. Better pack it in and go back to whatever part of the former USSR you come from.

VALYA: Are you finished?

JOHN: Yeah. Go on. Take your best shot. Lemme have it.

(Umberto the concierge hurries on.)

UMBERTO: *(Icily.)* Si, *Don* Martelli?

FRANCO: Please do not call me that...

VALYA: I would not waste my best shot on someone like you.

UMBERTO: I have forget, escuzi. Of course what I am meaning to be saying is: Si, Grand Signore Martelli?

FRANCO: I have already told you I am sorry, Umberto!

VALYA: I have a reservation...

UMBERTO: *Che cosa dici?* Now you are sorry! Big Mister Martelli is sorry...

FRANCO: *(Getting angry.)* Si! I am sorry!

UMBERTO: That's what you say!

JOHN: I was here first.

FRANCO: It's what I am! If I say I'm sorry, then I'm sorry!

UMBERTO: Ha!

FRANCO: Ha?

VALYA: Please, signores...

UMBERTO: That's right, that's what I say to you: Ha!

FRANCO: You say: Ha?

UMBERTO: Si. I will a say it again: Ha!

JOHN: I have a reservation...

FRANCO: So! You say: Ha! twice to me?

UMBERTO: Si! I say it twice! I say it thrice! Ha!

FRANCO: Three times you say this to me???? You say: Ha! three times in front of this nice honeymoon couple from Chicago???

JOHN: Whoa, there! We're not...

VALYA: Honeymoon! You have made a…

UMBERTO: I say: Ha! in front of his Holiness! I say: Ha! in front of God! Escuzi, honeymooners. *(Starting to take bags.)* We have a beautiful room for you with a nice big…

JOHN: Hey! Let go of that!

VALYA: I beg you, stop!

UMBERTO:…balcony overlooking the piazza and a nice bottle of Asti chilling in a bucket right next to the…

JOHN: Asti! Are you insane???

UMBERTO: *(Who has by now collected all the bags.)* Who is telling you this, signore?

JOHN: Telling me…

UMBERTO: Was it this man? *(He gestures to Franco with Valya's purse.)* Mister High and Mighty Franco Martelli? Has he suggested to you that I am crazy?

JOHN: No!

VALYA: Of course not!

UMBERTO: Because I tell you, signore, signora, that I am not crazy!

JOHN: My head is going to explode.

VALYA: May I please go to my room??

FRANCO: Mama mia, Umberto!

FRANCO: You say you aren't crazy and you act like this in front of nice honeymoon couple from Chicago???
(Valya and John collapse in frustration.)

UMBERTO: You call me crazy?? This man *(He points to John with purse.)* he don't like Asti and you call me crazy? I tell you what is crazy! I'll tell you…I'll…*(Umberto has finally noticed the purse.)* Hey, wait a minuto…whose is this?

VALYA: *(Wearily.)* Mine.

FRANCO: Give the nice lady her purse, Umberto…

UMBERTO: *(To Valya.)* This so-called purse, it's yours?

VALYA: Da…yes…si.

UMBERTO: *(Whirling to face John.)* Shame on you, signore!

FRANCO: Umberto! These poor people have come all the way from Chicago…

50 men's and women's scenes

UMBERTO: They have not!

JOHN: Finally...

UMBERTO: This woman is not your wife, signore!

VALYA: Not even close.

UMBERTO: You are no "honeymoon" couple!

JOHN: Bingo.

FRANCO: *(Interested.)* How do you know this, Umberto?

UMBERTO: *(Holding purse aloft.)* Elementary, Franco...this purse is a Russian knock-off of a Louis Vuitton...

VALYA: How do you know it is Russian?

UMBERTO: Simple, signorina! Look at the thread! It is the same military surplus thread the Russian army has been trying to sell on the black market all over Europe! It is the same horribly cheap and aesthetically displeasing thread that was used to hem your...whatever it is you are calling that...frock! *(Valya gasps and examines her hem.)* Had you actually been in Chicago, signorina, you would have undoubtedly gone shopping at Marshall Field where you could have gotten yourself decent attire or at the very least something that flatters your figure.

VALYA: What?!?

UMBERTO: Close examination of your clothing and belongings leads me to believe that you came here directly from Russia not O'Hare! This suitcase is a horrible knock-off, but one that is sold by the Russian mafia on every street corner in Moscow!

FRANCO: *(Gasping and crossing himself.)* Mafia! Oh, mio Dio!

UMBERTO: Si, la bella mafia! *(Whirling to John, who is laughing.)* And *you*, signore, seem to be wearing a silk suit from Hong Kong. From the look and smell of this recently purchased suit I would say that you've been wearing it...(He sniffs.) all the way from Hong Kong.

FRANCO: Aha!

JOHN: What's your point?

UMBERTO: My point, signore, is that since you have come here

directly from Hong Kong and since you, signorina have come
here directly from Moscow…

VALYA: Kiev!

UMBERTO: Whatever! The point is that you cannot possibly be
the honeymoon couple from Chicago and therefore I refuse
to allow you to cohabitate at this penzione!

VALYA: What??

UMBERTO: We are in the shadow of the Vatican for the love of
god! If you wish to sin, do it someplace else!

JOHN: You've made a huge mistake…

FRANCO: It is you who has made a mistake, signore! Here at the
Penzione Agrappi we do not offer shelter to gangsters!

VALYA: Gangsters?!?

UMBERTO: Nor do we offer honeymoon suites to couples living
in sin!

VALYA: We are not living in sin!!

UMBERTO: Ha!

FRANCO: Do not insult us, signorina.

VALYA: *Utcht ti chiort!* [Oh, you devil!] Give me my bags and call
me a taxi!

UMBERTO: Now she wants a taxi!

VALYA: This is your doing, Vittorio!

FRANCO: Vittorio?

JOHN: I had nothing to do with this!

FRANCO: Why does that name sound familiar?

UMBERTO: Your sister's cousin's husband.

FRANCO: Ah, yes…

VALYA: *(Struggling with Umberto.)* I want my bags!

UMBERTO: You want your bags? Take your bags!

> *(Umberto and Valya struggle to disentangle themselves.*
> *When the bags aren't immediately forthcoming, Valya grabs*
> *her purse from Umberto's hand and stalks toward the door.)*

VALYA: Have them sent to the Sheraton.

UMBERTO: *(Dropping all bags.)* Sheraton?!?

FRANCO: Sheraton?!?

VALYA: *(Whirling.)* Da! The Sheraton!

FRANCO: (Clutching his heart.) You would leave the Penzione Agrappi for the Sheraton??

UMBERTO: Traditore!

VALYA: (Advancing on the Italians.) Da! I would stay anywhere… even a Sheraton except this…this madhouse!

UMBERTO: Well, let me tell you something, Miss Moscow Mob…

VALYA: How dare you! You…you…

(A loud whistle from John silences the three and they all turn to see that he holds a large wad of lire.)

FRANCO: (Immediately solicitous.) Si, signore? What can I do for you?

UMBERTO: (Equally solicitous.) A nice cool drink, perhaps, after such a long journey?

(Valya begins to separate her bags from the tangled mess on the floor.)

JOHN: Gentlemen, I'm sure that we can all come to an…arrangement concerning the…young lady…

(Franco and Umberto are instantly transformed into models of discretion by John's liberal donation to each.)

FRANCO: (With an exaggerated wink as he counts his lire.) Si, signore. Think nothing of it!

UMBERTO: (Practically pushing Valya aside to pick up her bags.) Allow me, signora!

JOHN: (Tucking extra bills into Franco's pocket.) But we want to keep up appearances…

VALYA: I don't know what you think you are doing, Vittorio…

UMBERTO: Now, now signora. Signore knows best, si?

FRANCO: Of course, he does! Umberto, separate rooms for il signore and la bella signora!

UMBERTO: Si. (As he exits.) Lasciate ogni speranza, vol ch'entrate!

VALYA: Come back this instant!

JOHN: (Ignoring Valya.) What did he say?

FRANCO: (With a broad smile.) He says, he hopes that you and your lady have a most magnificent visit!

VALYA: *Lasciate ogni speranza, vol ch'entrate.* Abandon hope, ye who enter here. Dante. I want my bags!

FRANCO: Of course, Umberto is from the south, signora, His accent can be very difficult…especially for such a nice pretty signorina such as yourself.

VALYA: I will never stay here, signore! Do you hear me? Never!

FRANCO: *(As if she hasn't said anything.)* Now! You and the signore make yourselves comfortable right here while we make your rooms ready. I will have the girl bring you something to drink…some Chianti, perhaps?

VALYA: I want my bags!

FRANCO: Please, signora. No scenes, I beg you.

JOHN: He's begging you.

VALYA: I want my…*(Suddenly exhausted.)*…I have no idea what I want.

FRANCO: Anything, signora!

JOHN: Anything!

VALYA: Anything?

FRANCO: You have only to ask!

VALYA: My bags?

FRANCO: No! No bags!

JOHN: No bags!

VALYA: (Resigned.) No bags.

FRANCO: Absolutely not.

VALYA: Vodka?

FRANCO: Vodka?!?

VALYA: Umm…chianti, perhaps?

FRANCO: Ahhh! *(Calling.)* A nice glass…

VALYA: Bottle.

FRANCO: Bottle?

VALYA: Da. Bottle. I'll start with one.

FRANCO: I see. A nice bottle of chianti for Mrs…?

VALYA: Miss. Kormondov.

FRANCO: I see. If you will give me but a moment?

VALYA: I will.

FRANCO: Very good, then. Signore. Signora.

54 men's and women's scenes

(As Franco exits he indicates to John that Valya is a handful.)
JOHN: *(Chuckling.)* Wow. You gotta admit, that was classic. Did you see…
(John trails off when he sees that Valya is regarding him icily.)
Yeah. So…uh…I don't believe we've ever really met, have we?
VALYA: No.
JOHN: Right. Wow. Well…
VALYA: Well what?
JOHN: Well, here we are.
VALYA: *(Ominously.)* Da. Here we are.
RUBY: *(Entering.)* And that's how Prince John and Princess Valya first met.
(Blackout.)

Gunshy

Richard Dresser

Man & Woman

Evie (40) a woman trying to reconstruct her life following divorce and Carter (40) her current lover.

Scene: a home outside of Boston

> *Although she has a thirteen-year-old son, Jack, from her mar-riage to Duncan, Evie has become convinced that she and Carter must have a child. This effort has required the employ-ment of in-vitro fertilization. Evie and Carter have traveled to New England to celebrate Jack's birthday, and an unexpected blizzard has trapped them in the house where she and Duncan were once happy and in love. They are joined in this sorry situation by Duncan and his new girlfriend, Caitlin. Evie and Carter retreat to their bedroom where Carter prepares a shot of estrogen for Evie as he reveals his doubts concerning the future of their relationship.*

Lights up on a bed. Carter is in his pajamas with a hypodermic.

CARTER: What if they mixed up the sperm and you're carrying someone else's baby? I couldn't go through that again, Evie. *(Evie enters and starts to undress.)*
EVIE: There's nothing to worry about.
CARTER: There's always something to worry about.
EVIE: But what good does it do?
CARTER: It gives you an edge. Sometimes you can see what they're trying to do to you and you can stop 'em.
EVIE: Nobody's trying "to do" anything to you.
CARTER: Right. Everybody wishes everybody the best.

56 men's and women's scenes

EVIE: What's wrong?

CARTER: Nothing's wrong! *(Turning on her.)* Look, some days I work twelve, fourteen hours. I get on a roll and that's when they show me the money. You're saying you won't want me to cut back once we have a baby?

EVIE: Why would I interfere with your job?

CARTER: I start missing those big paydays I'm a wounded man. I *have* to close the deal. The bastards smell that and they walk away. So I get in my car and by the time I get out I'm just one more son of a bitch who's worried about his mortgage. I'm not going to let you do that to me.

EVIE: You think I want to take away your job?

CARTER: My parents split up when I was fourteen and I was on my own at sixteen. I know what it takes to get by.

EVIE: I don't know what you're talking about.

CARTER: You wanted a baby, so you found me. Once you have your baby, what do you need me for?

EVIE: You're afraid I'm going to leave you?

CARTER: I'm not afraid.

EVIE: Carter, I want you in my life.

CARTER: For now.

EVIE: Forever.

CARTER: That word doesn't mean a thing. They should ban it. Maybe it isn't even me you want.

EVIE: What do you think I want?

CARTER: You keep after me for this and that and I get to thinking you're trying to turn me into someone you could spend your life with, but that person isn't me. I'm very good at anticipating things.

EVIE: Which is probably why they happen.

CARTER: Has anyone ever left *you*?

EVIE: Actually, yes, in college.

CARTER: Jesus Christ. College. Your parents are still together. You're on speaking terms with everyone in your family. What the hell do you know?

EVIE: I don't know who you are right now.

CARTER: I'm a survivor, that's who I am.

EVIE: Even survivors run out of time, Carter.

CARTER: See? You even want to take that away from me.

EVIE: I thought I was giving you something.

CARTER: People who take always think they're giving. *(Beat.)* Come on, I'll give you the shot and we can go to bed.

EVIE: I don't think so, Carter.

(Evie leaves. Lights fade on Carter with the hypodermic.)

I Love You, Baby

Albert Verdesca

Man & Woman
Brie (20's) a hooker and Slice (20's) her pimp.

Scene: a dark street down by the docks

> *Slice made a fatal mistake when he hurt Brie's little boy. Here the vengeful hooker makes him pay.*

○ ○ ○

SLICE: Where was you last night?

BRIE: Last night?

SLICE: You heard me.

BRIE: I wasn't here last night.

SLICE: You got that right, bitch.

BRIE: My kid was sick. I had to take him to the doctor.

SLICE: A friend of mine said he seen you on the south side working a solo.

BRIE: I wasn't on no south side. I told you, I took my kid to the doctor.

SLICE: Ain't no doctor got hours that late at night.

BRIE: I took him during the day. I stayed home with him at night. He's just a kid. He needs me.

(Slice takes out a razor and menaces her with it.)

SLICE: I'll be checking that out. You better not be shittin me.

BRIE: You're my man, Slice. I'd never do nothin behind your back.

SLICE: You know you got a real pretty face. I'd hate to see it messed up.

BRIE: I swear I'm not shittin you.

SLICE: You know you the best of my womens, babe.

BRIE: I know that honey.

SLICE: You can't never leave me, Brie. You ever try anything funny and I'm gonna come after you and your boy. I'll find you wherever you be and you gonna be sorry the first day you laid eyes on me. You understand where I'm comin from? *(She nods.)* If I catch you lyin about last night, I'm gonna come after your boy and fix him so he ain't never gonna be able to make you a grandmother.

BRIE: Don't you talk about hurtin my boy.

SLICE: You don't want to hear me talk no shit, you better do what you suppose to. I pays your rent. I gets you out of jail. I gives you good spendin money. What kind of respect do I get for that, huh? I take care of you when your in trouble. I'm your man.

BRIE: Please put that razor away. You're scarin me.

SLICE: You better be tellin me the truth bout last night or your boy gonna suffer.

BRIE: I'm tellin ya the truth, now put that blade up.

(He closes the razor blade and puts it in his pocket.)

SLICE: Damn! Now you got me all worked up, girl. (He runs his hands over her body.) I think it's time to do what you do best and take care of your daddy.

BRIE: Sure, Slice. Where you parked.

SLICE: Don't need the car. Just step out the light— *(He takes her arm to lead her into the shadows.)* give me some of that good head.

(She pauses.)

BRIE: Let me freshen up my lipstick.

SLICE: Don't make me no difference what you got *on* your lips. It's what you gonna have between them that's important.

BRIE: I gotta look my best for my man.

SLICE: Well hurry up. I don't like waitin.

(She reaches into her purse and takes out a gun. She aims it at Slice.)

BRIE: I'm not doin it, Slice.

SLICE: Where the fuck you get that gun?

BRIE: I'm not doing it ever again.

SLICE: You lost your mind, bitch. Give me that gun.

60 men's and women's scenes

BRIE: Stay the fuck away or I'll shoot.

(He takes the razor out of his pocket and opens it.)

SLICE: You done overstep your bounds, girl. I'm gonna have to cut you 'cept you put that gun away right now.

BRIE: I'm leaving you, Slice. I was gonna wait a few more weeks 'til I saved more money but you caught me.

SLICE: You *was* working the south side, you motherfucker.

BRIE: For two months. Saved a lot of money too, not having to give you any.

SLICE: You know I'm never going to let you get away with this.

BRIE: You don't have a choice.

SLICE: You out your fuckin mind.

BRIE: I'm taking my boy away from all this. We're gonna start a new life in another city as far away from this as we can get. Maybe I'll find a husband and have more kids. You'll never touch me or beat me again and you'll never, never hurt my boy again. It only took that one time when you broke my boy's finger that I knew I had to kill you. I just didn't know when but this seems like as good a time as any.

SLICE: You ain't gonna kill me.

BRIE: Oh, yes I am. You're scum, Slice. Garbage. You think anybody's gonna be sorry to see you dead? I don't think so. The biggest mistake you made, Slice, was hurtin my boy. Guess you never had a momma who loved you 'cause you never know what I'd do to protect my boy. There ain't nothin, absolutely nothin that means more to me in this life than that little boy of mine. Once you hurt him, I knew it was over. I hated your guts from that time on.

SLICE: They'll lock you up. You won't never see your kid.

BRIE: You don't get the picture. You hurt my son. You been beaten on me. You threatened me with a razor before and you are threatening me now. You take one step toward me I'm gonna shoot you in self defense and I ain't gonna run. I'm gonna wait right here after I call 911, then I'm going to take care of sending my boy somewhere safe until all this shit blows over.

SLICE: *(Lunging at her.)* You motherfucker. *(She fires once into his stomach stopping him.)* Don't shoot no more, baby. I won't hurt you.

BRIE: Too late, you bastard.

SLICE: Call an ambulance. Hurry up.

BRIE: You won't need no ambulance. You'll need the undertaker.

SLICE: Baby, I'm sorry I hurt your boy. I'll make it up to you.

BRIE: *(Angry.)* What kind of animal would break a three-year-old's pinkey? What kind of man would hurt an innocent little boy? Huh? Why don't you tell me? Huh? You fucking coward, pimp. You piece of shit. *(He lunges at her in desperation. She fires into his chest. He dies. She takes a step up to him, surveys the body.)* Asshole. *(She fires one more time into the body then puts the gun down. She takes a lipstick out of her purse and applies it. She then takes out a cell phone and dials 911.)* I need the police. I just shot a man who attacked me with a razor. *(Pause.)* No. He's dead.

(Fade to black.)

In Search of the Red River Dog

Sandra Perlman

Man & Woman
Denny (20's) a frustrated husband and Paulette (20's) his wife, a woman mourning the death of her child.

Scene: a trailer home in Deerfield, Ohio. August, 1978

> *The mysterious death of their daughter has irrevocably divided Denny and Paulette. Denny desperately needs Paulette to return to his bed and she, in turn, has a desperate need to understand why their child has died. Here, they meet at night on the common ground of their garden and try their best to communicate these needs.*

> *At rise: The moon casts a cool light on a backyard ringed by an anemic looking garden, some rusted lawn chairs, a trash can and empty clothesline. Paulette slips out of the back door of the trailer wearing a nightgown. She playfully bounces her flashlight around as she inspects the painted glow-in-the dark rocks by the door and around her garden.*

PAULETTE: Mary, Mary, quite contrary, How does your garden grow? With silver bells and cockle shells…*(Pauses, flashes the light into the garden and picks up a beer bottle.)* And one beer bottle right in the middle! Denny? *(Tosses the beer can noisily into the trash can.)*

DENNY: *(Denny yells from inside the trailer.)* Who's that?

PAULETTE: Peter Peter Pumpkin eater had a wife but couldn't keep her! *(Stumbles into a trash can.)*

DENNY: *(Turning on a light in the trailer.)* Paulette?

PAULETTE: Put her in a pumpkin shell…

DENNY: Why don't you just wake up the whole damn neighborhood and we'll have a party!

PAULETTE: Oh, Denny please come out here and see our beautiful garden.

DENNY: It's the middle of the night.

PAULETTE: Pretty please with a cherry on top!

DENNY: Let me put my damn pants on, thank you. Which reminds me—

PAULETTE: That you love me?

DENNY: You are wearing some clothes out there aren't you?

PAULETTE: Of course, silly.

DENNY: Decent clothes?

(Paulette runs to put on a big volunteer fireman's jacket hanging up.)

PAULETTE: Lots of them.

DENNY: Well that's something.

PAULETTE: Now hurry before you miss the moon.

DENNY: Miss the moon! Jesus, I married one crazy woman. Miss the moon.

PAULETTE: Little Miss Muffet sat on her tuffet eating her curds and whey. Along came a Spider and sat down beside her and frightened Miss *(Overlapping.)*

DENNY: DAMN! Ouch! Owww. Just who put these damn rocks right in the middle of my feet?

PAULETTE: Are you hurt?

DENNY: I'm just fine, except for a few broken toes, thank you.

PAULETTE: I am so sorry.

DENNY: So it was you.

PAULETTE: Just hold on to me and sit down here.

DENNY: Could you tell me why you put all those rocks out here?

PAULETTE: I thought we could paint them with that glow paint and put them all along the garden path. I tried some already and I put them by the door to dry.

(Denny hobbles over to where Paulette is shining the light on the shining rocks.)

64 men's and women's scenes

DENNY: And I walked right into them, thank you.

PAULETTE: But look at them. Aren't they wonderful?

DENNY: They sure are different?

PAULETTE: You'll see how nice they'll look when I'm finished. It will look just like a ring of fire!

DENNY: And you want to put more of these out here?

PAULETTE: Oh yes. I want them the whole length of my garden.

DENNY: Paint them all different colors, huh.

PAULETTE: As many as they have. I just used what my parents had left in their garage.

DENNY: And put them along this...wonderful...garden.

PAULETTE: Exactly!

DENNY: Why honey?

PAULETTE: So they would be pretty. And we could see them from the road when we walked home at night—or look down at them from our window when we can't sleep. It would be special. A ring of fire.

DENNY: It would be different.

PAULETTE: So what do you think?

DENNY: To be honest?

PAULETTE: Yes?

DENNY: They just look like painted rocks.

PAULETTE: Well they are rocks on the inside. They will always be rocks on the inside. But we can make them into something special on the outside and—I would do it myself. It wouldn't cost anything much, I promise.

DENNY: I know you would do it Paulette, I just don't know why.

PAULETTE: If you love me, love me true. Send me a ribbon, and let it be blue. If you hate me, let it be seen, send me a ribbon, a ribbon of green.

DENNY: God knows I love you honey.

PAULETTE: Then you have to try to understand.

DENNY: Like why you're wearing my fireman's coat...with not much on underneath I see when I have told you over and over that it's not safe around here.

PAULETTE: There's no one living near us. No one for miles. To see us, or hear us…or visit.

DENNY: It wasn't two weeks ago Carter Brown's sister was taken right from her front yard—in the middle of the afternoon. Paulette, it was daylight. And you know what they did to her.

PAULETTE: Everyone knows I belong to you. You told me that the very first time you kissed me. You took my breath away when you kissed me. You're mine forever, you said.

DENNY: Jesus, Paulette, you don't forget anything.

PAULETTE: I'm Denny's girl. That means something.

DENNY: Not as much as it used to.

PAULETTE: No one would dare hurt me.

DENNY: Some things a man can't stop.

PAULETTE: Those dressed in red and blue have lovers so true.

DENNY: Things change.

PAULETTE: Those dressed in green and white—are forsaken in the night.

(Denny comes and holds her tightly.)

DENNY: There's animals out there. Animals with no names.

PAULETTE: Shhhhhh!

(Denny pushes Paulette to the ground and pulls out a small gun from his pocket.)

DENNY: Who's there?

PAULETTE: It's just an old owl. I hear him all the time.

(Denny gets up and goes to put the gun back in his pants as Paulette takes off the fireman's coat and hangs it back up.)

DENNY: Hell, just took five years off me. Can you beat that? Ready to shoot the shit out of an old owl.

PAULETTE: I thought you got rid of that.

DENNY: What honey?

PAULETTE: I thought we decided you were going to get rid of that gun.

DENNY: I'll get rid of mine when they get rid of theirs.

PAULETTE: That's not what you said.

DENNY: Soon as I get back to work and we get a decent place to live, then I'll get rid of it. Hell, I'll even let you throw it away. But right now I got to have one.

PAULETTE: Cross my heart and hope to die, cut my throat if I tell a lie. *(Paulette holds up the flashlight on her face.)*

DENNY: Hey, baby, you're going to cut yourself on that old rusted thing. Get yourself some of that lockjaw and the next thing I know I'll be all alone. I couldn't stand being that. So tell me, just what are you growing in this beautiful garden.

PAULETTE: Spices.

DENNY: Spices.

PAULETTE: Here's some for tea.

DENNY: Which I don't ever drink, thank you.

PAULETTE: And some for cooking.

DENNY: Macaroni cheese and beans, thank you twice and they don't need spice.

PAULETTE: Shhhhhhh.

DENNY: Buying food with those damn coupons makes me sick. They look at you like shit under their shoes when they can see they're not going to be getting any real money. I hate it.

PAULETTE: It's just temporary, honey.

DENNY: You having a job is temporary—like this garden. When we move I'll get you a big yard and you can plant what you want.

PAULETTE: I thought it might be nice to grow something right from the beginning. You know—where you can watch the seeds grow from scratch and nobody can take it away from you. I thought it would be nice to do together. I thought you would like it.

DENNY: Nice is having a job, or a wife waiting for you…nice is not having some damn dried up old plants in front of an old dump of a sardine can.

PAULETTE: Specks on the fingers, Fortune lingers; Specks on the thumbs, Fortune comes.

DENNY: There's still a fortune to be made working those mills, Paulette! I know I can outwork five of those Japs or Germans. I got three generations of steel men in my blood.

men's and women's scenes 67

PAULETTE: The plant's closed, Denny.

DENNY: That's just temporary, baby.

PAULETTE: That's not what they're saying in the newspapers.

DENNY: Aw, hell, Paulette, I told you not to read those lies. Those newspaper people don't give a damn about me or John Senior or you or Bertie. They just talk us down—make us out to be stupid and lazy fools or worse. We need those jobs and they know it. It's not us that doesn't want to work. Without those jobs we're nothing and they know that too. They want to break us, right back down to our hands and knees, but that's not the way we're going. We can't let them win and they know that too. But you're not going to hear the truth from them—and you're NOT going to read it in their newspapers cause those people are not on our side. Never were and never will be.

PAULETTE: I hate when you talk that way Denny. It scares me.

DENNY: I talk the way it is.

PAULETTE: You make it sound like war.

DENNY: It is war. The one who wins—wins everything.

(Overlap.)

PAULETTE: But it can't—

DENNY: And the one who loses—

PAULETTE: Denny…

DENNY: Loses.

PAULETTE: Maybe we could just pick up and move away from here.

DENNY: Why?

PAULETTE: Maybe we could start all over again someplace new.

DENNY: Where?

PAULETTE: Maybe I could go to college.

DENNY: *(Pause.)* Oh. That again.

PAULETTE: Just for two years.

DENNY: I'm still the steel man around here, aren't I?

PAULETTE: I read about getting a degree and I would promise to work really fast.

DENNY: You do believe in your steel man, don't you?

68 men's and women's scenes

PAULETTE: Of course I do, yes, always, but I really don't mind working.

DENNY: No, "buts" about it cause either you trust me or you don't. I either know what's happening or I don't. And I know, believe me, I go to the meetings. They're gonna take care of us. Both of us. All of us. Where are you going?

PAULETTE: I'm going in now.

DENNY: I'm telling you they have to take care of us.

PAULETTE: Cock-a-doodle dooo!

DENNY: Paulette!

PAULETTE: My dame has lost her shoe.

DENNY: Why don't you believe me?

PAULETTE: My master's lost his fiddle stick and knows not what to do.

(Denny swings her around and stops excitedly.)

DENNY: Honey we invented steel and rubber, radio, TV and every other fucking thing the world has that's any good. We are the center of the universe. We have to be.

PAULETTE: I'm cold.

DENNY: No wonder. You're not wearing enough to keep a fly warm and don't start telling me about how flies don't need to keep warm, thank you. *(Denny holds her very close.)* Now that's a whole lot better than any fly will ever know.

PAULETTE: *(Pulling away.)* I gotta go in now and finish reading my books. They're overdue tomorrow.

DENNY: I thought you might stay up and watch a little TV with me.

PAULETTE: We can't afford any more fines, Denny.

DENNY: Don't you think I know what we can't afford.

PAULETTE: Oh, Denny, I'm, sorry.

DENNY: *(Overlapping.)* No. I'm sorry, Paulette.

PAULETTE: Forgive me.

DENNY: No, it's always me, losing my head, shooting my mouth off.

PAULETTE: —Shhhhhh—

DENNY: I love you, baby. I'll always love you.

PAULETTE: I know. *(Pause.)* I'm just feeling so scared.

DENNY: I'm scared too. Scared you and me are never gonna be close again like we need to be. Like I want to be. Like you use to want to be.

PAULETTE: I just need a little more time, Denny. *(Pulling away.)*

DENNY: Don't you see me growing' old right before your eyes? Am I so bad to look at now you can't even stand being close to me?

PAULETTE: Please, you promised.

DENNY: 'Cause I remember it was different. I remember that and I know you can remember it too. If you wanted you could remember too, Paulette.

PAULETTE: I need more time! You know what the doctor said.

DENNY: And what do I need? What did the doctor say about me?

PAULETTE: Just a little while longer. I promise.

DENNY: Just so long as I know that you really love me.

PAULETTE: Don't be silly.

DENNY: Just so long as you don't start thinking about someone else. I couldn't stand that.

PAULETTE: You know there's no one else.

DENNY: Someone in your head…in those books…

PAULETTE: There's no one. No one but you.

DENNY: Okay. A little more time. *(Starts to leave.)*

PAULETTE: You know all those stars are always moving.

DENNY: What?

PAULETTE: Even though we can't see a thing they are and fifty thousand years from now it won't even look like the Big Dipper.

DENNY: Fifty thousand years from now I won't give a damn.

PAULETTE: It's so beautiful sometimes it makes me want to cry.

DENNY: Television makes you cry.

PAULETTE: You used to love learning all about the stars.

DENNY: When did I love it?

PAULETTE: When you had that science class in the twelfth grade.

DENNY: I didn't love learning about the stars when I had science class in the twelfth grade.

70 men's and women's scenes

PAULETTE: You did. You wrote that whole paper on it. I remember. You showed it to me. I read it. Every word of it and it was all about the stars.

DENNY: I didn't learn about the stars.

PAULETTE: You got a "C" Plus and Mr. Leebow—

DENNY: I bought it!

PAULETTE: What?

DENNY: I paid Chrissy Abbott to write the paper for me.

PAULETTE: You didn't.

DENNY: I did pay Chrissy Abbott to write that damn paper for me. I don't know one of those up there from the other. I never did and I never will.

PAULETTE: You paid her money?

DENNY: She was the smartest girl in my class and she said yes.

PAULETTE: But you only got a C-plus!

DENNY: I paid her to write a C-plus. Hell, if she wrote like an "A" paper, he would have known it wasn't me who did it.

PAULETTE: I thought you liked the stars.

DENNY: You liked the stars and I liked you, Mr. Leebow liked the stars and he liked you, but I didn't like him and I couldn't give a damn if the stars were moving or standing still.

PAULETTE: They are moving, but we can't see it. Why did you say Chrissy Abbott was the smartest?

DENNY: She was only the smartest girl in my class. You were the smartest girl in the whole school and Eric Vincent was the dumbest boy—but I was sure runner-up.

PAULETTE: You weren't dumb.

DENNY: The only difference between me and Eric was that he played the tuba and I could get my head beat in on the football field. That made me a lot more exciting. I mean, you weren't too interested in the tuba were you?

PAULETTE: Don't talk like that. You could be anything you want to be.

DENNY: You could be anything you wanted to be. I could be your boyfriend.

PAULETTE: I used to know all the constellations by heart. I could name them and draw them too.

DENNY: You were so smart—

PAULETTE: I knew all the stories about them.

DENNY: Smart and hot.

PAULETTE: Wonderful stories made up for each star. I could tell them all to you.

DENNY: Why'd I want to learn about the stars when I have you to tell them to me?

PAULETTE: They're wonderful stories. Like that one up there.

DENNY: The Big Dipper.

PAULETTE: You do know them.

DENNY: Everyone knows the Big Dipper.

PAULETTE: I like Ursa Major better. It's so much more mysterious to say "Ursa Major." And anything that's been sitting up there for maybe a million million years should be very mysterious, don't you think?

DENNY: Ursa Major.

PAULETTE: See, you are interested. In the winter the Little Dipper is to the left of the Big Dipper and has its handle pointed up while the Big Dipper's handle points down.

DENNY: It's pointed the other way.

PAULETTE: In the summer they change positions.

DENNY: Nothing stays the same.

PAULETTE: Do you know how far away they say those stars are?

DENNY: Further than Carlisle, Pennsylvania?

PAULETTE: Don't be funny.

DENNY: So, Miss World Book—how far away are they?

PAULETTE: They say the nearest one of those stars in Ursa Major is twenty-five millions of miles away from us. Imagine that. Twenty-five million miles.

DENNY: You're right. That's a helluva lot further than Carlisle, Pennsylvania.

PAULETTE: And we can still see it. Isn't it amazing? How bright it is.

DENNY: But not as bright as you?

72 men's and women's scenes

PAULETTE: And the brightest one of all, the one I've always loved the most, that's it right there at the end of my finger. See it?

DENNY: The one that almost looks like it's blinking?

PAULETTE: It's called Sirius, the Dog Star and it's the brightest one in the whole Northern Sky. Sirius, the hunting dog. So strong and so bright that if that star died tonight we'd still be seeing it for the next eight years.

DENNY: Maybe it's already dead.

PAULETTE: What?

DENNY: You just said it could be dead and we'd still be seeing it so I just said maybe it's already dead and we don't know it.

PAULETTE: I don't know.

DENNY: So it could be dead is what you're saying.

PAULETTE: I'm not sure.

DENNY: Hell, all this astrology business isn't so tough after all.

PAULETTE: It's not astrology, it's science. That's what makes it so special. A world full of laws that keep us moving and apart—moving and alone—moving and safe. All of those planets in their own little paths, and all of those millions of stars all part of this wonderful plan that keeps us planted on the earth and all of them up there dancing in the sky. It's a wonderful plan, a mysterious plan you could spend your whole life trying to figure out. And we're right there in the middle of it. I tell you it just takes your breath away.

DENNY: But if the law says it could be dead—it could be dead and I could be right. Right?

PAULETTE: Yes, I guess you could be right.

DENNY: No guessing about it. Now let's just go in and see some TV and find out what else old Denny can be right about.

PAULETTE: I'm not tired.

DENNY: You just said you were cold.

PAULETTE: I am cold. But I'm not tired.

DENNY: You never sleep anymore. People can die from not sleeping you know. I read that in the Reader's Digest.

PAULETTE: I'll come in soon.

DENNY: Forget all this junk about what's up there and help me work on what's down here.

PAULETTE: I'll be right in. I promise.

DENNY: It doesn't change anything, you know. Knowing every fucking name—it doesn't change anything unless. Unless— unless you could hook one of those bastards up to our electric line! Now that would change something. Hook that sucker up so we could quit paying a dime and you got something you can live with all right.

PAULETTE: It doesn't work that way yet.

DENNY: It doesn't work that way yet! (Pause.) That was a little joke, Paulette, maybe something Mr. Sweetass Leebow might like. I'm sure he liked your jokes a lot more than he liked mine. Fact is that he probably liked everything about you a helluva lot more than he liked me.

PAULETTE: He was just my science teacher, Denny, nothing more. He was—

DENNY: —a man! That is what at least, I think he was.

PAULETTE: He tried to help you. I don't know why you want to make fun of him. He never knew you didn't do that paper. Neither one of us knew that. I think he would be really sad if he found that out now because he believed in you. He believed in me.

DENNY: He believed in you. He tolerated me.

PAULETTE: He believed that we could be better. Smarter. He thought I could be a teacher.

DENNY: I'll bet he did.

PAULETTE: Why are you acting like this?

DENNY: I am no different than I always was. You were always the one with your head in the clouds, not me. And not now. Now I got my hands full figuring out what's happening down here! I got my head full of trying to make a living for the rest of my life and not end up a drunk like half the other old men I worked with. Hell, my head's so full of what's going on down here I don't even care anymore how those damn astronauts take a piss and God knows that was the only burning science question ever on my mind. (Pause.) Hello, Houston? This is Denny Griffith up here in Ohio and I've always wanted to ask how those astronauts took a piss? Sure, I can wait. How long? Doesn't matter you see, cause I don't have anywhere to go, or anything to do, so why don't you just put me on fucking hold like the rest of the—Paulette, what are you doing now?

(Paulette grabs the rake and works the dirt.)

DENNY: I need you, Paulette. I can't wait until some doctor says you can need me because he doesn't know what I need. He doesn't love you like I do. He doesn't know what I need.

PAULETTE: I married a wife on Sunday.

DENNY: Please be my wife again.

PAULETTE: She began to scold on Monday.

DENNY: Damn you!

PAULETTE: Middling she was on Wednesday.

DENNY: Damn you to hell! *(Exits to trailer.)*

PAULETTE: Worse she was on Thursday. *(Lights on in trailer.)* Dead she was on Friday. Glad I was on Saturday. To bury my wife on Sunday.

L'Eboueur Sleeps Tonight
(for worlds are destroyed by day)
Jerome D. Hairston

Man & Woman
Little John (30's) a high school English teacher and Amber (17) his student and clandestine lover.

Scene: here & now

> *Little John has been sleeping with Amber, but has recently fallen in love with a prostitute. Here, he breaks off his relationship with the tempestuous teen.*

○ ○ ○

AMBER: Don't try to spare me. Just give it to me straight. What's her name?

LITTLE JOHN: Who?

AMBER: My replacement. The one you're meeting after school tomorrow.

LITTLE JOHN: You're not being replaced.

AMBER: Is she pretty?

LITTLE JOHN: You got it all wrong.

AMBER: A cheerleader. Barbie doll legs. Breasts like soup bowls.

LITTLE JOHN: Soup bowls?

AMBER: She go to our school? Some bimbo from another period?

LITTLE JOHN: What do you think I am. Some greedy pervert with a Lolita complex?

AMBER: Who's Lolita?

LITTLE JOHN: Look, you're the only one I'd take this chance with, believe me.

AMBER: Then why get rid of me? Is it something I did? Cause I can change.

76 men's and women's scenes

LITTLE JOHN: It's not you that has to change.

AMBER: It's the way I dress, isn't it? My Cabbage Patch wardrobe. It's my Mom, I'm telling you. Look, underneath these rags is one sophisticated lady. I can refine myself. Whatever it takes. I can be whatever she is to you.

LITTLE JOHN: You don't mean that.

AMBER: Why don't I?

LITTLE JOHN: Because she's a prostitute.

AMBER: A what?

LITTLE JOHN: I went to a prostitute.

AMBER: What does that mean?

LITTLE JOHN: It means a whore. A professional.

AMBER: So she's better in bed. I understand.

LITTLE JOHN: What?

AMBER: This isn't class you know, you don't have to speak in metaphors.

LITTLE JOHN: I'm not speaking in metaphors. I'm trying to tell you the truth.

AMBER: Well, then do it. Just say you're seeing someone else.

LITTLE JOHN: How can I see someone else? I don't even see myself anymore. Look, sometimes you have to destroy yourself. So you can see the pieces missing. And fill them.

AMBER: I'm confused.

LITTLE JOHN: I know what I have to be.

AMBER: What's that?

LITTLE JOHN: A teacher. *(Pause.)* Look, I can't make you understand.

AMBER: No you can't.

LITTLE JOHN: I can't make this any easier on you.

AMBER: No, you can't.

LITTLE JOHN: But I can't keep seeing you. *(Silence.)* Not like this.

AMBER: So, I'm supposed to forget the last three months. To sit in class and hear you drone on about pronouns and prepositional phrases. To put all that meaningless drivel in place of all the tender things you've said to me. The way you make

men's and women's scenes 77

me feel. The way you touch me? That's what I'm supposed to do?

LITTLE JOHN: Wait a second, you think I drone?

AMBER: I didn't mean it that way.

LITTLE JOHN: Meaningless drivel? Is that what you get from my class?

AMBER: That's not my point.

LITTLE JOHN: No, it's all the point. Look what I've done to you.

AMBER: You haven't done nothing to me.

LITTLE JOHN: See, there. Double negative.

AMBER: So?

LITTLE JOHN: So, I've deprived you. You supposed to be in school to learn. Not daydream about me.

AMBER: It's only English, Jimmy.

LITTLE JOHN: Only English? It's the cornerstone of communication. Without everything we say we would have no meaning. You'd be lost in the world. It's my responsibility that doesn't happen to you. And by distracting you, I haven't done my job.

AMBER: A distraction. Is that what you think this is?

LITTLE JOHN: No.

AMBER: Neither do I. I know you don't want to hear this, but I don't give a shit about English. You say I'd be lost without it. Well, I've understood every word and I'm as lost as I've ever been. Look in my eyes.

LITTLE JOHN: I am. Believe me, they're what I'm going to miss most. The strange way they fill up with me. Amazed that you can conjure something good. But I haven't earned the image. It's time I did.

AMBER: You don't have to leave me in the process.

LITTLE JOHN: I can't live with the secret, Amber.

AMBER: Then let's not make it a secret.

LITTLE JOHN: What?

AMBER: What if everyone knew?

LITTLE JOHN: What would that do?

AMBER: You tell me.

LITTLE JOHN: It would ruin me. Is that what you want to do?

AMBER: I want you to be with me, and I'm just saying, I'm willing, to do, whatever, to make that happen.

LITTLE JOHN: Don't do this, Amber.

AMBER: Would it be that bad? To have me next to you? Would you be that ashamed?

LITTLE JOHN: No one's ashamed of you, Amber. But you're only...

AMBER: A kid? Is that what you were going to say? That I'm too young?

LITTLE JOHN: No.

AMBER: Too ugly?

LITTLE JOHN: No.

AMBER: Not experienced enough. Don't satisfy you enough?

LITTLE JOHN: Not at all.

AMBER: Then what's stopping us?

LITTLE JOHN: It's not that simple.

AMBER: What's more simple than two people giving up everything cause they love each other? That's as true as it gets right? And can truth be a bad thing? All it takes to make this work is for you to love me. And you love me, don't you? (Pause.) Don't you?

LITTLE JOHN: It's not that I don't love you. Believe me that would make all the difference in an ideal world. But we live in one full of contradictions, lies and discord. I'm not saying what we had wasn't special. But at times you got to make sacrifices so that something special can remain untouched. I don't want to taint it. If we can recognize the magic for what it is, it'll make the pain of moving forward, letting go, more tolerable. This is the right thing here, trust me. Now, was there anything wrong with what I just said?

AMBER: No, everything you said was beautiful. Except for one thing.

LITTLE JOHN: What?

AMBER: In the beginning. When you said you loved me.

LITTLE JOHN: Yeah?
AMBER: You used a double negative.
   (Silence.)
AMBER: How about that, Jimmy I'm learning.

The Maiden's Prayer

Nicky Silver

Man & Woman

Taylor (30's) a man coping with tragedy, and Cynthia (20's-30's) his wife.

Scene: a grand house in the country

> Everything seemed perfect for newlyweds Taylor and Cynthia; big beautiful house in the country, a good job and baby on the way. When Cynthia miscarries, they discover that their relationship lacks the depth to carry them through this tragedy together. Here, the grieving couple shares an uncomfortable moment together several months after the miscarriage.

○ ○ ○

> The lights come up on the yard and the back of the house. Taylor is seated on the grass, trying to assemble the tricycle. Cynthia appears in the doorway. Her composure is firmly in place.

CYNTHIA: What are you doing?

TAYLOR: Do you know that there are no words on these instructions?

CYNTHIA: What?

TAYLOR: There are no words, just drawings with letters and arrows. This piece slides into that piece, slides into this piece, slides into that piece. It's a nightmare. Who do they think is putting these things together?

CYNTHIA: What are you doing?

TAYLOR: Trying to finish the tricycle.

CYNTHIA: Why?

TAYLOR: It's no use like this.

CYNTHIA: But there's no one to ride it. *I'm* too big to ride it.

TAYLOR: I know that.

CYNTHIA: You're too big to ride it.

TAYLOR: I realize.

CYNTHIA: Why are you making it?

TAYLOR: Cynthia—

CYNTHIA: Do you think it's going to rain?

TAYLOR: Don't you want to try again?

CYNTHIA: Try what?

TAYLOR: It's been four months.

CYNTHIA: I just don't understand why you're putting that thing together. You should take it back.

TAYLOR: I can't take it back.

CYNTHIA: Don't you have the receipt?

TAYLOR: Months have passed.

CYNTHIA: Since what?

TAYLOR: Since I bought it.

CYNTHIA: I bet they'd take it back anyway. I bet they would, if you told them what happened.

TAYLOR: Why would I do that?

CYNTHIA: So they'd take it back. Am I speaking Chinese?

TAYLOR: Cynthia—

CYNTHIA: *(Disturbed.)* You use my name too much.

TAYLOR: I want a child.

CYNTHIA: Can we talk about something else? I was reading a magazine the other day, or maybe it was a book, it was all about these people, I can't remember the details. Did you read it?

TAYLOR: I want a child. Don't you?

CYNTHIA: *(Correcting him.) Another* child.

TAYLOR: Alright.

CYNTHIA: Don't pretend things didn't happen. Things happened.

TAYLOR: I know they did.

CYNTHIA: Opportunities get missed.

TAYLOR: Why don't we make love anymore?

CYNTHIA: We make love.

TAYLOR: We haven't.

CYNTHIA: Don't be silly.

TAYLOR: Not since way before—

CYNTHIA: We make love all the time. Why just last night—that wasn't you? I'm sorry—I'm just kidding.

TAYLOR: We should make love.

CYNTHIA: Oh why?

TAYLOR: We're married.

CYNTHIA: That's the best you can do?

TAYLOR: I love you.

CYNTHIA: We make love. We do. Just not that often. Once say, maybe twice a year. That's as much as lots of people. I bet there are people who never make love. I bet there are people who go through their whole lives and never touch another human being. Blind people, fat people, nuns.

TAYLOR: It's been four months.

CYNTHIA: I know. You said that.

TAYLOR: I want to hold you.

CYNTHIA: I want to go away.

TAYLOR: I want to taste you.

CYNTHIA: I want to go to London.

TAYLOR: I want to be inside of you.

CYNTHIA: Have you ever been to London.

TAYLOR: No—

CYNTHIA: When I was a little girl my father took me to London. I loved it. All the money is different colors. It's wonderful!

TAYLOR: I want to make love to you.

CYNTHIA: *(Snapping.)* Well, you have to understand! You just have to understand. And wait!

TAYLOR: *(After a beat.)* Maybe you should talk to someone.

CYNTHIA: *(Pleasant again.)* I'm talking to you.

TAYLOR: Someone else.

CYNTHIA: Well, I spoke to *Libby* today. She called. She called to check up on me, to see "how I'm doing." It's so insulting.

TAYLOR: I meant a professional.

CYNTHIA: Libby's a professional. She's a prostitute.

TAYLOR: You know what I mean.

CYNTHIA: And I think prostitutes have to be very good listeners. That's what they say, on all the talk shows. The men come to them and pour their troubles out, all over the bed. And the whores have to be very sympathetic, and understanding and good listeners. I'm sure it helps if they're good lays too.

TAYLOR: Fine.

CYNTHIA: I'm sorry.

TAYLOR: Would you like to go to London?

CYNTHIA: You don't want to go to London.

TAYLOR: Maybe we should.

CYNTHIA: We can't afford to go t o London.

TAYLOR: We should get away.

CYNTHIA: Don't give in to me.

TAYLOR: What do you want!?

CYNTHIA: You know what I want.

TAYLOR: …Oh.

CYNTHIA: I never even saw him.

(There is a long pause. They just look at each other. He returns to his work.)

TAYLOR: The instructions don't have any words so I can't be sure I'm looking at this right side up.

(She starts to leave, but stops at the door.)

CYNTHIA: *(Softly.)* Don't you ever want to hit me?

(He turns around, shocked by her question, but she is gone. The lights fade out.)

84 men's and women's scenes

Marcus Is Walking
Scenes From the Road
Joan Ackerman

Man & Woman
Michael (20-30) a man lost and in a hrurry, and Ellen (20-30) his
wife.

Scene: the simplest possible car

> *Here, a young couple bickers as they try to find the house to
> which they have been invited for dinner.*

○ ○ ○

> *Michael and Ellen, in their late twenties/early thirties, are
> equally anxious. Michael—dressed in corduroy trousers,
> worn button-down Oxford shirt and tie—drives too fast,
> leaning forward, holding the steering wheel tightly. Ellen,
> dressed up nicely in skirt and sweater, clutches the arm rest.*

ELLEN: We're not lost.
MICHAEL: *(Thinks they're lost.)* No.
ELLEN: We're not.
MICHAEL: Great.
    (Pause.)
ELLEN: Could you please slow down?
    (He doesn't. She grips her seat.)
ELLEN: Michael, it's seven twenty-eight. We're not late yet.
MICHAEL: *What* are we looking for?
ELLEN: A rotary. They're having cocktails first and then dinner.
    We're not late.
MICHAEL: We're not late we're not lost, we're on the wrong
    road.
ELLEN: We're not on the wrong road.

MICHAEL: We're on the wrong road.

ELLEN: We're not on the wrong road.

MICHAEL: What's the name of the road?

ELLEN: What road?

MICHAEL: The road we're supposed to be on.

(Pause.)

MICHAEL: Well?

ELLEN: I don't know.

MICHAEL: Ellen, *you* got the directions. You're supposed to know what road we're supposed to be on.

(Pause.)

ELLEN: What road are we on?

MICHAEL: We're on Route 9 east.

ELLEN: That's the road.

(He glances at her.)

Ellen We're supposed to be on. If you don't believe me, stop and ask that man.

MICHAEL: Ask him what?

ELLEN: If this road goes to a rotary.

MICHAEL: No.

ELLEN: Why not?

(Michael turns the wheel.)

ELLEN: *(Lurching.)* Michael, you're going to spill the soup.

MICHAEL: What soup?

ELLEN: The soup in the back.

MICHAEL: There's soup in the back?

ELLEN: I made soup. It's a potluck.

MICHAEL: What's a potluck?

ELLEN: The dinner we're going to. Is potluck. Everybody brings something to eat. A dish.

MICHAEL: *(His tension mounting.)* That's *insane*. What if everybody brings the same thing?

ELLEN: They don't. Michael, lighten up.

MICHAEL: What kind of soup?

ELLEN: Pea.

MICHAEL: Pea soup?

86 men's and women's scenes

ELLEN: Yes, pea soup.

    (Pause.)

MICHAEL: They know you're bring pea soup?

ELLEN: I told Pauline I'd bring pea soup.

MICHAEL: Who's Pauline?

ELLEN: Pauline is the wife of the head of the English department. The man who hired you. The man whose house we're going to.

MICHAEL: Or not. *(Pause.)* Did she ask you to bring soup, any kind of soup, or specifically pea soup?

ELLEN: She asked me what I wanted to bring and I said soup.

MICHAEL: So she doesn't know it's pea.

ELLEN: No.

    (Pause.)

MICHAEL: It seems a little…

ELLEN: What?

MICHAEL: Well. Mundane.

ELLEN: It's not mundane. It's delicious. It's full of herbs. Herbs de provence.

MICHAEL: Ellen, this is a very…high-powered department. These guys are into hermaneutics. Deconstruction.

ELLEN: Michael, *please* slow down.

MICHAEL: This is the wrong road.

ELLEN: Well, you're going to end up farther down the wrong road faster.

MICHAEL: I'm turning around.

ELLEN: Fine. Be late.

    (He pulls over, stops, idling the car.)

MICHAEL: Let me see the directions.

ELLEN: You won't be able to read them.

MICHAEL: Let me see them.

    (Reluctantly, she hands him an envelope with sketches on it.)

MICHAEL: I can't read a word of this. *(Pointing.)* What is this?

ELLEN: It's the sycamore tree. We turned at.

MICHAEL: This says sycamore tree?

ELLEN: It *is* a sycamore tree.

(He stares at her.)
MICHAEL: What is this?
ELLEN: Michael, I don't like you tone.
MICHAEL: Ellen, this party is for me. This dinner party is for me, this potluck event is an opportunity for the whole department to meet me and I'm not there and they are.
ELLEN: No, they're not. They're not all there yet.
MICHAEL: What does this say?
ELLEN: That's the bluegrey house we turned left at. Those are columns. On the front porch.
MICHAEL: Why can't you write down directions in English?
ELLEN: They're symbols, Michael. Symbolism.
MICHAEL: We turned here? At this house?
ELLEN: Yes, we turned left there.
MICHAEL: And then what did we do?
ELLEN: We turned right at the fire station.
MICHAEL: *(Trying.)* Fire station?
ELLEN: On the right side of the page means turn right, on the left, left.
MICHAEL: I can't... *(Highly frustrated.)* Where is north? Ellen?
ELLEN: Huh?
MICHAEL: Where is north?
ELLEN: You're being obnoxious. North on the envelope or north out there?
MICHAEL: North on the envelope. I know where north out there is.
ELLEN: I don't know.
(He hands her back the envelope. Puts his face in his hands.)
MICHAEL: I'm gonna lose my job. My reputation is already shit before I even start.
(Ellen watches someone walking by.)
ELLEN: Let's ask her.
MICHAEL: *Who*?
ELLEN: Her.
MICHAEL: Her? That woman? *(As if Ellen's insane.)* Ask her what?
ELLEN: If there's a rotary up ahead.

88 men's and women's scenes

MICHAEL: No! No! Don't ask her anything!
(She rolls down the window. He abruptly pulls back onto the road.)
ELLEN: Excuse me! Hi, excuse me, is there a rotary up along this road?
(They speed away. Ellen leans back in.)
ELLEN: Why do men never ask for directions? Why don't they? What is it? Why are you incapable of asking a friendly stranger a friendly reasonable question that that person has had themselves many times?
MICHAEL: That's horrific grammar.
ELLEN: What do you have to hide? You can't admit for one second of one day you're just a little bit unclear, a little bit hazy about your whereabouts, what is so terribly embarrassing about that? You'd ask somebody what time it is, why can't you ask them where a particular geographic location is, it's not like we're in a war zone, you're divulging the whereabouts of your troops, Michael, if you don't slow down I'm going to leave you. I swear, I am not going to be married to someone who drives like a maniac and is insensitive to my feelings.
MICHAEL: *(In a panic.)* If I can't make it to dinner on time, how am I going to make it to class on time, that's what they're wondering. That's what they're saying right now to each other over their pots and their luck. Jesus Christ, you never wanted me to take this job. You didn't want to move here. You didn't want to leave New York. That's why you didn't write down the directions intelligibly. That's why you made pea soup!
ELLEN: *God*, I hate the way you drive!!
MICHAEL: I hate the way you ride!!
ELLEN: I would ride better if you would drive better!!
MICHAEL: I would drive better if you were capable of writing down directions!!
(Silence. Tension.)
ELLEN: *(Thrilled.)* There it is!
MICHAEL: What?

ELLEN: The rotary. Take a right, here. Quick, now.

MICHAEL: Edmund Street?

(He takes a right.)

ELLEN: Second driveway.

MICHAEL: He lives on Edmund Street?

ELLEN: Right here. This driveway here. Wisteria on the mailbox.

MICHAEL: 103? Is that what she told you, 103?

ELLEN: Park by the dumpster.

MICHAEL: Why do they have a dumpster? You're sure this is the right house.

ELLEN: They're putting on a new roof.

MICHAEL: A new roof?

ELLEN: It's constructive deconstruction.

MICHAEL: Oh my god, there's Rafferty, I can see him through the window. Oh…god…

ELLEN: See? They're still having drinks. We're not late. *(Lovingly.)* Take a deep breath.

MICHAEL: Okay. *(Takes a quick shallow breath.)* Okay.

(He turns off the motor. They both get out of the car. He puts on an old worn tweed jacket he grabs out of the back window while she opens the back door and gets the soup.)

MICHAEL: How do I look?

ELLEN: You look great.

MICHAEL: I look okay?

ELLEN: Yup. Professorial.

MICHAEL: You have the soup?

ELLEN: I have the soup.

(He comes around and kisses her quickly on the lips, looking at Rafferty in the window. Moves ahead. Stops. Turns, looks at her. Takes a breath, really taking her in. Moves back to her and gives her a meaningful kiss. Takes the soup from her and starts to go.)

ELLEN: Michael? *(He looks back at her.)* Which way is north?

MICHAEL: *(Pointing.)* That way.

(She looks that way as he goes ahead.)

ELLEN: Hunh. *(Impressed, to herself.)* Pretty good. *(She follows him.)*

90 men's and women's scenes

The Pharmacist's Daughter

Monika Monika

Man & Woman

John (20-30) a pharmaceutical salesman, and Becky (20's) a pharmacist's daughter; a woman with unusual assets.

Scene: a backyard in Fruitport, Michigan

> *Unwittingly, John has been pressured by Harry, a pharmacist, to spend some quality time with his beautiful daughter, Becky. On the eve of Clinton's inauguration, John and Becky find themselves alone at her home. After a round of idle banter, the sinister implications of Harry's deal with John are revealed.*

○ ○ ○

> *A suburban back patio, on a clear, cold, snowy night. John and Becky are adjusting a large tower TV satellite dish. From the window we see a static big screen TV, the presidential inauguration plays. They struggle with the satellite dish.*

> *John looks at her. The tension is thick. He takes a deep breath, inhales. It's cold, they've got coats on.*

JOHN: What's that smell?
BECKY: Smell?
JOHN: *(Inhales again.)* It's very musky.
BECKY: Oh that.
JOHN: What is it?
BECKY: Fear.
　　(He smiles and then turns his attention to the satellite dish.)
JOHN: I'm not sure I know how to fix this thing.
BECKY: I'm not that hot on watching the inauguration.

JOHN: Yeah?

BECKY: Yeah.

JOHN: Yeah?

BECKY: Yeah.

JOHN: You like my way with words, I can tell.

> *(He reaches over and cups his hand behind her neck. She stands stock still. Heavy sexual tension throughout, they're a little punch-drunk on each other. They kiss. It's a great kiss. They end up lying in the snow.)*

JOHN: I don't do this. I usually, I wait. You know, it's so crazy out there.

BECKY: Mmm hum.

JOHN: But this is amazing. I feel like I know you. Listen, it's like everything that's coming out of my mouth is a cliché from every bad movie…

BECKY: I like it. There's sincerity in clichés. In fact I prefer clichés to clever things, because they're more honest, you don't have to think to say them, you just feel and out it comes. I don't want anybody seducing me with anything but clichés from now on.

JOHN: That's what's so wonderful about you. I never say the word " wonderful." I feel so comfortable, like I can say anything. It just feels right.

BECKY: It does.

JOHN: Hi.

BECKY: Hi.

> *(John gets up and walks to an old swing set.)*

BECKY: Bye?

JOHN: Becky, I have to tell you something.

BECKY: Oooh. Interesting.

JOHN: I'm serious. The reason I came here.

BECKY: *(Smirking.)* To watch the "inauguration."

JOHN: It's weird, but, it's about Harry and, things I sold him…

> *(She loses her confident smirk. She steps away from him.)*

BECKY: *(To herself.)* I don't believe this.

JOHN: What?

92 men's and women's scenes

BECKY: No, go ahead.

JOHN: It's about...Harry.

BECKY: Go on.

JOHN: He. He sort of. I agreed to stay here...this is strange, I mean like I've been set up but...

BECKY: *(A hint of a smile is emerging.)* Uh huh.

JOHN: I sort of agreed to come here tonight in order to make a sale. To your father. I made a deal...but I'm not sure what the deal is exactly.

BECKY: Jesus.

JOHN: I'm sorry. It's just that I'm surprised—I like being here so much, and I want to get the record straight. I promised. God, I guess I promised Harry I would come here, but that I wouldn't...get involved with—with you, I guess. Does this make any sense to you, because it doesn't to me...
(John waits, wondering what it is on Becky's face.)

BECKY: What are you some kind of monk? Some kind of last of the honest people breed? Are you some kind of idiot?

JOHN: What the hell are you getting mad about? It was Harry that...

BECKY: I mean what do you think you are? I don't know what the fu...*(She starts to march indoors. John grabs her and stops her.)*

JOHN: Hey. There's something going on here. What's going on here?

BECKY: *(Blurts it out.)* Harry and I have a deal is what's going on here.

JOHN: A "deal?"

BECKY: Yeah. I stay here, I get lonely, I need someone, he gets them, with a big sale. He brings them here when I can't stand being here alone anymore.

JOHN: What?

BECKY: And it's not really a problem, Mr. John Gorajick, that is when the price is paid and the deal is done, so tell me what the hell you think you're doing by going back on the deal with my father.

JOHN: The "deal."

BECKY: Yes. You come here one night and then you leave. And then the next quarter, we go again, Mr. Gorajick.

JOHN: Wait a minute. Whoa. You tell me, Ms. Becky, why the hell a woman like you needs to have her father pay to bring a man home. I don't get it.

BECKY: Because I can't leave Fruitport, okay?

JOHN: Not okay. What does that have to do with it?

BECKY: Harry and I have an arrangement. I stay away from the men in Fruitport—the young people don't stay in this dump, they leave and get a life. In exchange, he brings me home his traveling pharmaceutical salesmen.

JOHN: But why would he have given anyone a big sale, or anything to be with you?

BECKY: He doesn't pay them to come here—he pays them not to stay.

JOHN: He pays them to go away.

BECKY: Yes, and they never stay, even if they say they are, and sometimes they come back for a couple of quarters, they disappear and that's how it works.

(John sits on a teeter totter. It drops to the ground with a soft thud.)

JOHN: Tell me why can't you leave here.

BECKY: No. I won't tell you. Who do you think you are? Shit! You wrecked it.

(Becky kicks the swing set, slips and falls into the snow. She lands hard and starts to cry.)

JOHN: *(Goes to her, comforting her.)* Hey, hey, hey, hey, hey, hey. *(Becky lunges up and embraces him. Almost pulling her down onto him. She's very different, the cool is gone, she's terribly vulnerable.)*

BECKY: Thank you.

JOHN: Whoa! What's this?

BECKY: God, thank you. You good, sweet John Gorajick. Thank you. You told me. None of them ever said anything, and I just watched them not telling me all the time they were here. You said it right like that.

(He holds her tightly, wondering if this girl might be crazy, but loving the closeness.)

JOHN: Come on. Let's go watch the inauguration.

BECKY: I want to make love to you. And I want you to talk to me and I'm going to touch you right on the inside of yourself.

JOHN: Oh, sweet. You're crying, look at this… Just, shhh…

BECKY: I'm so alone.

JOHN: Hey. I'll stay with you. Let's just slow down.

BECKY: *(Dropping all facades.)* Who are you? How did you come here? Please stay.

JOHN: For a while.

BECKY: I like you.

JOHN: Ditto.

BECKY: Ditto?

JOHN: I'm not any good with words…

BECKY: There's nothing devious about you, John Gorajick.

JOHN: I have to tell you, if you keep doing that, I'm not going to be able to resist you.

BECKY: I know.

JOHN: Are you okay?

BECKY: Just, put your cheek on mine. I want to feel it.

JOHN: Mmmmmm…

BECKY: Mmmmmm…

(John is truly getting worked up.)

JOHN: Oh, boy. Okaaaay.

(He goes in to kiss her. Becky, suddenly playful pulls away.)

BECKY: I've got a secret, I'm dying to tell you, I haven't told anybody ever. Well, almost nobody.

JOHN: Now?

BECKY: It's very interesting.

JOHN: Okay. Tell me.

BECKY: *(Bursting, almost laughing.)* This is very important, I think you should know this, okay? Before we make mad passionate love in the snow. It's about me. About my body.

men's and women's scenes 95

JOHN: *(A tad annoyed.)* What? Herpes?

BECKY: Nope. Not even a cold sore.

JOHN: Good. No, I mean, is it anything like it? Better? Worser?

BECKY: Nope, nope, nope, nope, it's not like that.

JOHN: *(Getting into the playful mood.)* You're a homicidal maniac, some kind of serial killer?

BECKY: Uh uh.

JOHN: ...or—a man? *(Quickly, suddenly worried.)* I mean even if you're a man, the plumbing would be wrong, but I'm not completely... (Dreading the answer.) are you a man, Becky? *(She shakes her head, he's relieved.)* Good.

BECKY: It's about my breasts and what I've had done to them. Hardly anybody knows.

JOHN: They're not—real? I'm sorry. I mean, I'm not sorry they're not real, but...

BECKY: Oh, they're real.

JOHN: Good. I mean, silicone has proven not to be inert.

BECKY: I'm genetically engineered.

JOHN: Huh?

BECKY: Yeah. I was genetically engineered a few years ago, so that my breast milk contains useful proteins that can help people with crippling diseases.
(John laughs.)

BECKY: *(Hurt.)* Hey. Don't laugh.

JOHN: *(Laughing.)* I'm not. This is not laughing. This is nerves. I always do this when I'm nervous, it drove my father crazy. Okay. I'm not laughing anymore.

BECKY: *(Frowning.)* But you're smiling.

JOHN: *(Smiling.)* Not inside, I'm just interested and a little upset. It just looks like I'm smiling, I'm not. When I'm happy I cry, just a couple wires got crossed in my emotional circuitry. Really.

BECKY: You must be weird at, like funerals, and circuses and stuff.

JOHN: It's not that exact.

BECKY: But what if we go to a comedy someday?

96 men's and women's scenes

JOHN: Can we get back to, uh, what do you mean "genetically engineered," exactly?

BECKY: It's, like, just a cut and paste on my DNA. They take these attributes from DNA that can fight these diseases and insert it into my genetic code.

JOHN: Oh. Why?

BECKY: So that it can be expressed in my breast milk.

JOHN: That's wild, Becky. You're a complicated woman, aren't you?

BECKY: It's simple high school genetics.

JOHN: I missed that class.

BECKY: Well?

JOHN: How...do they get the...the milk? Can I ask that?

BECKY: That's really pretty unscientific and primitive.

JOHN: Which means...

BECKY: If I have sex and well, things happen and you might, well, accidentally...?

JOHN: Uh huh.

BECKY: That's why I'm telling you. I usually don't let anyone touch them. But it won't happen unless you're pretty rough. Like pretty, focused on...that. Are you rough on the breasts in sex?

JOHN: No. Sometimes. But rarely. But overall, sometimes. But not particularly now.

BECKY: How do you feel about a really gentle session. I mean, would you consider having a very gentle time tonight?

JOHN: You're telling the truth.

BECKY: Yes.

JOHN: I'm thirsty. You wanna drink of water?

BECKY: Oh. Oh. I see. You think I'm a freak now. Of course you would. I'm so used to it...

JOHN: No I don't think you're a freak.

BECKY: You don't think it's freaky that I'm genetically engineered?

JOHN: A little.

BECKY: Great.

JOHN: Wait a minute.

BECKY: You're looking at my breasts like they're freaks.

JOHN: No, you're wrong. I like your breasts. In fact, I've had a problem, the last few minutes thinking about anything but your breasts. When I met you this afternoon, that's why my chemicals went off the scale. I'm a breast man.

BECKY: A breast man? Tell me something. Where do men get off even liking breasts? I never understood it. I mean, legs, okay, or butts or vaginas these all have functions that help sex along, but breast are not even meant for you! Where did you men get the idea that breasts are for you? They're sweat glands. They're for babies—not men. You can't make me feel freaky about genetically altering myself to produce helpful microbes in my breast milk, because I did it to help all those people with Parkinson's and Alzheimer's, hemophilia, and emphysema, and to pay my student loan, My breasts make microbes and they're going to save people, my breasts are going to teach mankind how to eradicate the scourges of the twentieth century, so they're not for you, and your breasts are useless so why do you even have any?!!!

JOHN: Whoa! Wait a minute, wait a minute.

BECKY: No! You're being a redneck. Like provincial. You're afraid of technology and what's more you have my body so pegged, just for you, you're scared of my tits because they are milky and righteous and animal and you can't take it.

JOHN: *(Getting mad.)* Hey. No way, I surf the internet. I slept with a woman that could control the direction of her urine and I've tasted menstrual blood. Twice! I am a traveling salesman, I've been there.

(They look at each other: an impasse. She laughs. John looks like he's going to cry.)

BECKY: Are you okay?

JOHN: I'm laughing inside.

BECKY: Shhhhhh…

(It's a truce. They drift together, striking each other.)

BECKY: You'll just go away and I'll never see you again.

98 men's and women's scenes

JOHN: I'll see you again.

BECKY: I mean, you're not going to want to live in Fruitport.

JOHN: No, I'm not going to live in Fruitport.

BECKY: You promise you'll come back again, no matter what?

JOHN: Yeah, I promise.

> *(Curiously, he reaches over and unzips her coat. He lets a finger fall on her sternum, then considers.)*

JOHN: *(Cont'd.)* May I?

BECKY: You want to touch them?

JOHN: I want to touch you.

> *(She starts unbuttoning her shirt.)*

BECKY: Don't tell Harry. I shouldn't have told you about the deal.

JOHN: I can deal with Harry.

BECKY: What about the inauguration?

JOHN: What about the inauguration?

BECKY: *(Shivering.)* You're not nervous, are you?

JOHN: Suddenly, No. How did you know?

BECKY: You're not smiling anymore.

> *(Lights start to fade.)*

JOHN: Come here.

BECKY: Do you like?

> *(She opens her coat for him.)*

JOHN: You're beautiful, you're so beautiful, I can't even tell you...

BECKY: Thank you. They're patented.

> *(Lights are out.)*

JOHN: What?

Plunge

Christopher Kyle

Man & Woman

Matty (30's) a charming ne'er-do-well, and Val (30's) the woman
he thinks he loves.

Scene: a restored farmhouse in Western Connecticut

> *When these two college chums are reunited at a weekend
> gathering, married mom Val shocks devoted Matty by reveal-
> ing her interest in another woman.*

○ ○ ○

*Late Saturday night. The living room. Matty is smoking a
cigar, pouring over the baby pictures. Val comes downstairs
and watches him. Beat.*

MATTY: That was a long nap.
VAL: Where's Clare?
MATTY: Sun porch.
VAL: I need to talk to her.
    (The others laugh offstage.)
MATTY: They're trying to draw Jim out—childhood traumas or
    something. It's not for the squeamish. What do you want to
    talk to her about?
VAL: *(Smiling.)* Girl stuff.
MATTY: You realize whatever you tell her will get back to me
    eventually. She's very bad with secrets. *(Val coughs pointedly.)*
    Your husband gave it to me. *(Puts out the cigar.)* You know
    I'm sorry about before. I'm always jealous of your success.
VAL: Success?
MATTY: The Con Ed job. I bet it's a great opportunity. I'm only
    mean to the people I love, have you noticed that?

100 men's and women's scenes

VAL: That's not true; you're mean to lots of people.

MATTY: Well, all right, if you want to be picky. *(Holds up a photo.)* This is my favorite.

VAL: I look terrible in that one.

MATTY: Yes, but look at Harris holding the baby. Have you ever seen him so competent? I mean, his contribution to the miracle of life amounted to what—two minutes of grunting? But he's standing there like—

VAL: Nicholas adores Harry. With me, he starts screaming and shaking the second I pick him up.

MATTY: I doubt that.

VAL: I never got the glow, Matty. New mothers are supposed to have this instinct that takes over and you just *know*. What to do. Nicholas can tell I don't have the glow.

MATTY: I'm sure you're an amazing mother. Probably read every book there is.

VAL: *(Beat.)* I used to have more confidence, you know. Sometimes I catch myself looking for it—like if I wear a certain five-year-old jacket, maybe I'll... *(Shrugs.)* I'm in a transitional period.

MATTY: Tell me about it.

VAL: Is this priest thing for real?

MATTY: My mother decided I'm too old to be such a fuck-up.

VAL: You'll find something. One of these days.

MATTY: Not if I don't look.

VAL: It'll be a woman, I think. Underneath you're just a squishy romantic.

MATTY: You're not really going to quit your job, are you?

VAL: Probably.

MATTY: That disappoints me. I know—I should talk—

Val. You really shouldn't—

MATTY: But I rely on you, Val. You give me depth by association.

VAL: You are *so* not amusing me right now.

MATTY: I mean it. My whole universe is going to come crashing down when you start defending nuclear power.

VAL: I'm not defending nuclear power.

MATTY: And Clare's going to be worse off than me.

VAL: Clare will be fine. Clare is always fine.

MATTY: She'll love you no matter what. But she'll love you more if you don't quit.

VAL: Doesn't she just infuriate you sometimes? I thought we were having a quiet weekend—I mean, what's with—

MATTY: I think she invited us to cushion the blow. When she dumps that poor Jim, she's going to be very down on herself.

VAL: You always think the worst of people.

MATTY: And I'm usually right.

VAL: I think it's just the opposite: she really likes Jim and she wants us to get used to him.

MATTY: No way.

VAL: You think they're sleeping together?

MATTY: How else would they meet?

VAL: She's so beautiful, anybody would jump at the chance…I can't understand why she always ends up with—

MATTY: Losers? Clare's like Malibu Barbie slumming it on the Island of Misfit Toys. For an hour or so she graces the less fortunate with her luminous 36-18-36 presence. But then Ken drives up in a pink dune buggy and Malibu Barbie speeds away with a wistful wave and a shower of sand.

VAL: *(Laughing.)* You're too mean.

MATTY: Trust me, Jim's about to get his shower of sand.

VAL: I really miss her.

MATTY: Yeah.

VAL: But when I do see her I never feel like I'm happy enough. She wants us to be happy, Matty.

MATTY: I'm just the opposite, I draw such strength from the suffering of others.

VAL: Especially mine.

MATTY: You married him. *(Beat.)* So, haven't you noticed? I'm being nice to Harris this weekend.

VAL: You are?

MATTY: He's a very underrated guy. Excellent taste in cigars.

VAL: I hate him.

MATTY: Okay…

102 men's and women's scenes

VAL: I can't believe I said that—I didn't mean it.

MATTY: You're going to leave him?

VAL: Of course not. He'd stay up all night trying to figure out what side of the bed to sleep on. I talk for him at parties, you know; he gets his thoughts all constipated. He wouldn't even crack a book if I didn't— But mostly he's sweet, don't you think? I want to stay with him, I really do. Because when you get right down to it, how many people can you count on?

MATTY: We never should've split up, huh? *(Val laughs.)* What?

VAL: Going out with you—that had to be the most absurd thing I ever did.

MATTY: Okay, I'm wounded.

VAL: Matty—we fought all the time.

MATTY: We love to fight.

VAL: It got old.

MATTY: That's why you dumped me?

VAL: Come on.

MATTY: No, really. I want to know.

VAL: You were obviously more interested in Clare.

MATTY: You knew that?

VAL: Everyone did. Except maybe Clare.

MATTY: Poor, dim Clare.

VAL: You're still—

MATTY: Oh, no. No,

VAL: How many dates have you had this year?

MATTY: I can't really count. Three.

VAL: Three?

MATTY: I did sleep with one. She's very cool—sings for this punk band called That Barton Fink Feeling.

VAL: So what happened?

MATTY: Oh, I didn't see her again. She had these incredibly long toes, like talons. Frightening. As soon as she took her shoes off I wanted to leave. But I went through with it, you know, for the sake of her feelings.

VAL: You are so neurotic.

MATTY: It's not neurosis. It's my child-like belief in perfection. You have beautiful feet, by the way.

VAL: Thanks. *(Matty tries to kiss her. She pulls away.)* Matty, come on. Christ.

MATTY: I'm sorry. It was just an impulse. *God. (Beat.)* Are you sure? I know I'm not attractive or terribly nice or even good in bed, but—

VAL: Matty, just stop, okay?

MATTY: Harris won't notice, I promise.

VAL: I've been seeing a woman.

MATTY: *(Beat.)* Okay—it sounded like—

VAL: Yeah. I've been seeing a woman. *(Laughs.)* Sounds weird. I've been dying to tell somebody.

MATTY: Wow. I mean, Jesus. On the one hand, you know, I'm totally shocked, but also strangely aroused.

VAL: Try not to say anything stupid.

MATTY: Of course not.

VAL: I have no idea what I'm doing.

MATTY: Right. Look, I don't know how to respond to this. You always know what you're doing. Are you really gay or are you just trying to be hip?

VAL: I don't know, I don't know, I don't know.

MATTY: Do I know her?

VAL: Piper Almond.

MATTY: Piper? I hate her.

VAL: Because she wouldn't go out with you?

MATTY: She told you? *(Val nods.)* Can you really be serious about someone who'd betray a confidence like that?

VAL: Who says it's serious? But for the time being—

MATTY: She's much too shallow for you, Val. It's like dating a personal shopper.

VAL: She's really funny—

MATTY: She isn't.

VAL: She reads my mind, in a way. We actually have conversations where I'm not explaining every other thing I say.

MATTY: Does Harris know?

VAL: Are you *high*?

MATTY: Listen, Val, maybe you should leave him.

VAL: That's not going to happen.

MATTY: Wouldn't it be fun to hang together again—the three of us? And Piper, if you insist.

VAL: Give it up.

MATTY: Come on. Christ, why stay with Harris? *(She points to the baby pictures.)* Look, kids are very adaptable.

VAL: I don't expect you to understand, but when Nicholas cries at night I can't wake up anymore. Harry takes care of it. Always, and never says a word. I want him to yell at me, tell me how selfish I am…but he won't; he's very kind. It would kill me to hurt him. You don't always have to—love, I mean. There's just more to it than that. *(Pause.)* Sometimes I don't feel things the way I used to. Do you?

MATTY: I don't understand.

VAL: Then you're worse off than I am.

Polaroid Stories

Naomi Iizuka

Man & Woman
G (Zeus, Hades) and Eurydice (18-20's)

Scene: a pier at the edge of a city, the late 1990's, night.

> *Eurydice has stolen quietly into the underworld. When she attempts to rip-off a sleeping Hades, the god awakes and reveals his broken heart.*

○ ○ ○

> *G and Eurydice— eating the fruits of the underworld.*

> *The sound of breathing, a heartbeat. G is sleeping. Eurydice is going through his pockets carefully. She finds matches, paper, an orange—nothing of value to her. She searches for a watch, no watch. She sees a charm around his neck, starts to pull. G grabs her hand. Eurydice breathes in—the sound of a girl taking a breath before diving underwater.*

G: girl, what the fuck are you doin?
    (Eurydice extricates herself.)
EURYDICE: i wasn't doin nothin.
G: you think you gonna steal from me?
EURYDICE: baby, don't flatter yourself. you ain't got nothin to steal.
G: steal my soul.
EURYDICE: i don't want to steal you soul, old man.
G: steal my heart.
EURYDICE: i don't think so.
G: steal my little good luck charm. yeah? you like that, huh? fourteen karat gold.

EURYDICE: it's pretty. it's like something a girl wears.

G: baby, i ain't no girl.

EURYDICE: i know that. see, that's what i'm saying. i'm a girl. you could give it to me, and then, i don't know, i'd be like your girl or something.

G: you want to be my girl, huh? what if i don't want you to be my girl?

EURYDICE: hey, man, fuck you.

G: now, why you got to talk like that: "fuck you, fuck you"?

EURYDICE: i talk like i want. and i don't even want to be your girl anyway.

G: well, make up you mind, little girl.

EURYDICE: i don't want to be your girl, old man.

G: tss. you takin it the wrong way.

EURYDICE: i don't even know what you're trying to say.

G: i'm tryin to say, maybe things ain't always what they seem. i'm sayin maybe you got to look a little harder.

EURYDICE: i'm lookin real hard at you right now.

G: oh yeah? and what do you see?

EURYDICE: you old—

G: —uh huh—

EURYDICE: —but you ain't that old.

G: i ain't that old, i ain't that young. baby, i'm like a god
(G picks up the orange, and begins to peel it.)

EURYDICE: tss. man, i don't believe you're a god. you're too dirty and snaggle-toothed to be a god.

G: uh huh, well, maybe this god ain't that pretty. you think a god's got to be pretty all the time? you think he's got to smell sweet and shit gold? is that what you think?

EURYDICE: i don't know, i don't think about stuff like that.

G: yeah, i know that. that's cause you're young and dumb.

EURYDICE: man, fuck you.

G: "fuck you fuck you"

EURYDICE: man, what do you want from me?

G: for real? girl, i want a good night's sleep.

EURYDICE: that's it?

G: that's it.

EURYDICE: that ain't nothing.

G: now, that says to me, you ain't never had a good night's sleep—

EURYDICE: —tss—

G: a good night's sleep, that's a treasure. rest your weary bones, free yourself from all earthly cares. but now, i ask you, how can a man get a good night's sleep when his woman's got one eye open, waiting to rip him off, slit his throat. that ain't no way for a man to live. if a man can't trust, it'll drive him crazy, it'll piss him off, make him meaner than hell. here, you want some orange?

EURYDICE: no.

G: it's good.

EURYDICE: i don't want no fuckin orange.

G: it's good. florida orange, girl, fresh off the tree, here,

EURYDICE: man, you are so weird. i can't figure you out, i can't follow how you think. i can't get inside you head.

G: i like to be able to sleep easy.

EURYDICE: so sleep easy, baby. i ain't gonna stop you.

G: cant sleep easy unless you got some trust. i like to be able to give a person trust.

EURYDICE: tss. can't trust nobody

G: now that ain't true. anybody says that, they don't know, i feel sorry for them. if they can't trust, it's like they ain't even truly lived.

EURYDICE: man, that's bullshit. you got to watch your back all the time. everybody's runnin some scam, for real. everybody wants something. and some folks, it's like they can get it for free. they're all like, i love you, shit like that.

G: girl, why you got to talk like that?

EURYDICE: man, shut up

G: cause, see, love ain't shit. it's somethin real and pure and true.

EURYDICE: yeah, that's what they all say but that ain't even it, see. it's like they want to tell you how it is, tell you how it's gonna be, and they ain't even lookin at you. it's like they're lookin right through you like you was a ghost or something.

G: maybe they see somethin inside you, you don't even know is there yet.

EURYDICE: man, they see what they want to see. it's their own fucked up trip. ain't got nothing to do with me.

G: girl, you're talkin about love, right, and love is mental. even in the good times, it's gonna make you crazy, and in the bad times, i swear, it's gonna make you wish you could put a bullet through your brain, put yourself out of your own damn misery. and then when it's all gone you gonna wish you could do it all over again.

EURYDICE: man, for a god, you don't know shit.

G: yeah, yeah, yeah, i'm a fuckin fool for real.

EURYDICE: i'll tell you what i know, for real: don't let nobody get too close cause i don't care how nice somebody is, fuck nice, you let them get close enough, they'll take everythin you own, your own self even, ain't nobody who won't.

G: some will, some won't.

EURYDICE: tss. ok, you believe in love and all that shit.

G: yeah, i do.

EURYDICE: why? you got somebody you love, old man? you got some girl you love?

G: i used to.

EURYDICE: yeah, and what? she broke your heart? she take off, she leave you high and dry?

G: yeah, she broke my heart, but that was a long time ago, she was my lady love, she was my queen, and i loved her with all my heart. so yeah, i believe in love and all that shit.
(Eurydice tries to pick up the stuff she took from G and return it to him.)

EURYDICE: here, that's yours. i messed up all your stuff, i'm sorry.
(time slows down. G gives Eurydice a piece of orange, and she eats. he gives her another, and she eats. and as she eats, she transforms into something softer, something of who she used to be.)

EURYDICE: it's good. where i come from, there's these orange groves, all along the freeway, and the orange trees, they have these little, white flowers, all tiny and lacy like. man, i ain't even thought about this in so long. i used to go out there all the time, with this guy i used to know, this goofy guy i used to know, and sometimes we'd be out there, and there'd be this wind, and all the flowers, they'd start falling. we'd close our eyes, and laugh so hard. for a little while, nothin else mattered, and everythin was perfect, cause when the wind got up and the flowers started falling, it was like it was snowing, and the air smelled all of orange, and we thought it was so cool, we thought it was the coolest thing in the whole world.

(G caresses Eurydice like a god caresses a maiden. Orpheus slowly appears like a shadow of the past. Eurydice sees him. and the peace and tranquility is broken. the pulse begins.)

EURYDICE: look, i got to go, i got to get going.

(Eurydice resumes picking up G's stuff, and gives it back to him.)

G: you always going, huh? that must be a hard thing to always be going.

EURYDICE: sometimes, it's like if i can just keep moving, nothing bad'll happen, sometimes, it's like if i stop, i'll die.

(Eurydice goes.)

G: —hey, hold up. what're you afraid of?

EURYDICE: i ain't afraid.

G: what're you so afraid of?

EURYDICE: i ain't afraid of nothing.

G: that ain't true, i know it ain't. cause it ain't about love. it ain't even about that. you hear what i'm saying? ain't about nothin 'cept getting out alive.

(G takes out a knife.)

G: here.

EURYDICE: i don't want that. i don't want that.

G: girl, ain't nowhere left to run, ain't nowhere left to go, here, take it, go on—take it.

110 men's and women's scenes

Refrigerators

Judy Soo Hoo

1 Man & 3 Women

Crystal (30-40) an Asian-American woman searching for treasure in the past, Carol (30-40) her sister, Emiko (20's) their mother, a beautiful young woman coming of age in a Japanese internment camp in 1943, and Kato (20's) her husband.

Scene: an appliance store

> *Following their mother's death, Crystal and Carol search in an old refrigerator for her will. They discover instead an old journal, which reveals the mother they never knew: a young woman in love.*

O O O

CRYSTAL: This is it. the 1942 Westinghouse model. Let's open it up.

(Crystal pulls on the handle of a refrigerator, but fails.)

CAROL: Mom never threw anything out. It'll be weeks before we sort out the stuff in the house.

CRYSTAL: It's stuck.

CAROL: So?

CRYSTAL: Mom's will is in there.

CAROL: I know.

CRYSTAL: Don't you want to know what she left us?

CAROL: What she left you. You were her favorite.

CRYSTAL: And you were Dad's.

CAROL: So they're both gone. We can be friends now.

CRYSTAL: Go to hell.

CAROL: All right.

(Carol turns to leave.)

CRYSTAL: Wait! We need to get her will so her lawyer can settle the estate.

CAROL: So we can pillage the riches.

CRYSTAL: Absolutely.

CAROL: Then, here! I'll help you pull.

(Carol and Crystal both tug at the door handle. Still, stuck.)

CAROL: Dammit! Why couldn't she use the bank's security deposit box?

CRYSTAL: Goes back to the war, Banks froze all the assets of all the Japanese when they shipped them off to camp.

CAROL: Where did you learn that?

CRYSTAL: In college. Do you think that our parents would tell us anything about camp? It was war.

CAROL: We're not at war.

CRYSTAL: Who cares? Mom was a crazy delusional woman.

(They tug at the handle.)

CAROL: So am I.

CRYSTAL: Sorry. I didn't mean anything by it. Did you take your medication?

CAROL: Every day, Sister Woman. One blue pill a day deeps all the emotions at bay.

(The refrigerator door opens. They look through the refrigerator drawers.)

CAROL: Fire insurance, mortgage…Hey did you know Mom and Dad paid $1,500 for this tract house in 1947?

CRYSTAL: Good deal.

CAROL: Yeah, considering the hakujin neighborhood.

CRYSTAL: I have it. Her will.

CAROL: Great, let's go.

CRYSTAL: Wait, there's some more stuff.

(Crystal pulls out pictures, ribbons and medals.)

CAROL: Who cares? She never threw anything out. She even saved old coupons and buttons from our dresses.

CRYSTAL: Ribbons in the Japanese Tennis League. Medals from Church. Look Grandma and Grandpa Toshi! Mom in a bathing suit. First place in the breaststroke.

112 men's and women's scenes

CAROL: Look at her pert breasts, her slim waist and that face. Hey, she looked liked one hot Mama.

CRYSTAL: She was beautiful. She was nineteen.

CAROL: She didn't look as good when she died. Her skin was falling off her and she couldn't talk.

CRYSTAL: She didn't eat and she just stared out with those eyes that never seemed to blink.

CAROL: Hey, let's go. Who cares about that stuff? Who needs memories when you have television?

CRYSTAL: What's this? Looks like a journal and letters. *(Crystal begins to read.)* August 14, 1942.

(Emiko, a beautiful young woman, enters.)

EMIKO: The winds are hot; the dust jumps into our mouths. We spit sand on the harsh desert floor. The sand lodges in our hair, in our throats, in our armpits and between our legs. Our only relief is at night when we lay on our cots and not think of living in these barracks with a dirty green sheet separating families.

March 23,1943. Father thinks that the United States will lose the war. I don't care because Kato broke my arm. We were playing baseball and I was running into third when Kato threw the ball at my arm and tore up my elbow. I think I'm in love.

(Kato, a handsome young man, enters tossing a baseball.)

April 14, 1943. Kato and I got married. On our wedding night, we made our cots one. We were so nervous, we turned on the radio and listened to Hank Williams songs. In two days, Kato is shipping out to join the Army.

(Lights change to Crystal and Carol reading letters.)

CRYSTAL: Our mother got married after knowing Dad for three weeks?

CAROL: Isn't that romantic?

CRYSTAL: No. It's foolish. I'm getting married to Fred and I've known him for three years.

CAROL: They were in love. Read on.

CRYSTAL: June 16, 1943.

EMIKO: Kato sends me letters from camp every day.

(Kato dons a military uniform.)

KATO: Dear Emiko, I've learned how to peel potatoes and shoot an M-1. I've also learned how to bayonet. Thrust, thrust then plunge with a twist into the neck. We're shipping out to train in England then onward to Germany.

EMIKO: October 12, 1943. Ooh. A new transferee came into camp. He says nothing but he stares real long at the table where my friends eat mashed potatoes and beans. His name is Calvin and my friends point out his broad back that tapers into a V at the waist. But I have already noticed that.

December 24, 1943. At the Christmas festival, snow falls in tiny patches. Calvin and I dance with our arms far between us. We twirl, swing and dip. I feel the warmth of his skin through my hands and it makes me breathe like I've been running up a hill.

KATO: January 1, 1944. Happy New Year! I've gotten to know some of the guys in the outfit and they know that I'm one of them not one of those Japanese who are pillaging the Pacific. In England, it rains and the Germans shower us with bombs. We are being briefed in Italian and French, mon amour. I hope to see action soon.

EMIKO: Feb. 14,1944. Calvin brushed up against me, put his hand on my shoulder and then to the back of my neck then ran it down my spine to the small of my back.

(Emiko and Calvin kiss.)

KATO: April 29,1944. Emiko what have you been doing, lately? I haven't gotten a letter recently. In the air, there is a feeling of something happening soon. We are going to liberate Europe. It's been almost a year since our hasty marriage. I have your picture and take it out at night and put it under my pillow.

EMIKO: June 12, 1944. Is it possible to love two things and want two things? I like fish and rice, yet I can't live without either. I say this because Calvin has asked me to go to Chicago with him.

KATO: June 15,1944. Emiko, we will land in Italy at dawn, tomor-
row, Pray for me. I look at your picture every night.
(Lights change. Back to Crystal and Carol.)
CRYSTAL: I can't read anymore.
CAROL: You're stopping? Go on. You just got to the good part.
CRYSTAL: We're late and have to be at the lawyer's office.
CAROL: Read on! We still have some time.
CRYSTAL: I want to know what Mom left us.
CAROL: Now, you're interested in what Mom left us? She left us
this journal. Don't you want to know what happened?
CRYSTAL: Some things are better unknown.
CAROL: She was actually human. She was in love. That's so
romantic.
CRYSTAL: She's dead. It's the past. It's just history.
CAROL: Big sister, you don't have an imagination.
CRYSTAL: Oh, yes I do.
CAROL: Don't you want to know what happened?
CRYSTAL: No! I don't! Just leave it alone!
CAROL: Why?
CRYSTAL: I don't…I can't. Look, we have the will and the insur-
ance papers. We'll come back and read it.
CAROL: I want to know.
CRYSTAL: Just leave it alone for now! Leave it alone!
*(Carol nods. Crystal puts the journal and the letters back into
the drawer. Crystal and Carol start to leave. Lights change.
Crystal is back at the department store.)*
CRYSTAL: Some things are better left in the dark.

The Shiva Queen

Rebecca Ritchie

Man & Woman
Roger (30-40) a man grieving over his wife's recent death and
Shirl (30's) a professional Shiva organizer

Scene: the living room of a condo

> *Shirl has been hired by Roger's mother to organize his Shiva
> house following his wife's death from cancer. Here, the self-
> proclaimed Shiva Queen explains how she came to be in the
> mourning business.*

○ ○ ○

SHIRL: *(She consults her list. To Roger.)* I expect you'll want your
own *Yahrzheit* candle. The funeral home will bring a big one,
of course, but a lot of my Bereaveds find it a comfort to light
a memorial candle, even before the funeral. Helps them
sleep.—I'll just leave it in the bedroom.

ROGER: No, please!—I don't want anybody in there. In the bedroom. We spent a lot of time in there. All our time in there
the last two years. She didn't get up much.

SHIRL: I know what you're going through. I really do. I'm a
widow.

ROGER: You mentioned.

SHIRL: That's how I got into this business. When Mitchell died, I
said, "I thought I was prepared for anything." I thought there
was nothing that would catch me unaware. I take pride in
being an organized person.

ROGER: I've noticed.

SHIRL: But here this—thing—happens, and I completely lose it.
Can't find my way out of a room.—The laundry's piling up in

the basement, the food's turning green in the frig.—And there's nobody I can turn to. No family in town.

ROGER: *(Glancing toward den.)* Maybe you were lucky.

SHIRL: I'm wandering around after the funeral, the house crammed with people, feeling worse than I've ever felt in my life, and all I can think is I'm throwing the biggest party of my life, and I haven't even cleaned my oven.—I use Oven Quick in the green can. Ten minutes, and the enamel's like new.— So that's when it dawned on me.

ROGER: What?

SHIRL: This was my window of opportunity! I checked the Yellow Pages, and can you believe it? There was not a single person in the *shiva* business.

ROGER: I'm not surprised.

SHIRL: It's a great business. I get people's houses ready. Run their errands.—And it never gets boring. I love the challenge.

ROGER: Don't you find it depressing?

SHIRL: Oh, no! You meet the nicest people this way.

ROGER: Nice?

SHIRL: Well, needy. Ready to open up. You'd be surprised how responsive people get when they suffer a loss. At least, that's how losing Mitchell made me feel. That's one of the reasons this seemed such an ideal job. A chance to dress up, meet new friends…

ROGER: You make friends this way?

SHIRL: Well, not friends, exactly. People like you. Deeply responsive acquaintances. I find that by the end of a *shiva*, I'm emotionally linked to most of my clients.—Don't you feel we're becoming emotionally linked?

ROGER: I can't feel anything at the moment.

SHIRL: You will. You'll start relying on me.

ROGER: I don't really think this is a basis for lasting friendship.

SHIRL: You'd be surprised. My clients know they can call me any time…to talk, to get in touch with their feelings…

ROGER: How many…clients…have you had?

SHIRL: In the past three years…hundreds, easily.

ROGER: And you keep them all straight?

SHIRL: I start with file cards with vital statistics. Then I transfer it all to my personal computer: Age, hygiene, annual income, marital status.—And I update. I read the newspaper from cover to cover, especially the business pages, and of course the wedding announcements. And the obituaries. It's important to know who's still out there. Available. And might feel the urge to call.

ROGER: You *are* organized.

SHIRL: That's what people pay me for. They know I'll take care of everything. Any time, anywhere.

ROGER: Arlene took care of everything. Even with the doctors' appointments, and the surgeries, and the medication—she took care of everything.

SHIRL: At least you had some warning. With cancer, you always get some kind of hint.

ROGER: I didn't. I still can't believe it. I thought we'd beat it.

SHIRL: You had to, just to get through it. but underneath, you had to have a nagging doubt. Some suspicion it was terminal.

roger: I didn't. I believed them. The doctors.

SHIRL: What else could you do? Radiation, experimental drugs, bone marrow transplants.—You couldn't put a person you loved through all that without believing the doctors.

ROGER: I had such faith in them. It's an Oncology Center, for God's sake! They have to know what they're doing.

SHIRL: And they do. Within limits.

ROGER: Your husband...how did he—?

SHIRL: It was such a fluke. Right outside the synagogue. The one place you would think was risk-free.—He had Yahrzheit for his mother, or he wouldn't have been anywhere near the place.—An electrical storm comes up—lightning, thunder, trees uprooted everywhere. This huge branch falls on him, pins him to the ground.

ROGER: I'm really sorry.

SHIRL: And there I am, sitting at home like an idiot, waiting for my husband to get back for dinner, with the leftover sushi on the table and two glasses of plum wine—and I see the whole thing on the TV news.

ROGER: It must have been horrible.

SHIRL: Did I plan this?

ROGER: You can't plan everything.

SHIRL: *I* plan. Now, I *plan*. Nothing will ever catch me off balance again.

ROGER: I hope not.

SHIRL: I intend to foresee everything.

ROGER: You're more resilient than I am.

SHIRL: Method. That's the secret. Decide what you want out of life, and go after it. Step by step.

ROGER: I wish I thought I'd get over this.

SHIRL: You're better already. I can tell. You'll be ready for a relationship in no time at all.

ROGER: I'm never going to look at another woman. Arlene's memory will be sacred forever.

SHIRL: I'd reconsider that, if I were you. There are a whole lot of Saturday nights in forever.—Excuse me. I need your shoes.

ROGER: My shoes?

SHIRL: Mourners don't wear leather.

(She helps him remove his shoes and slips a pair of slippers on his feet.)

ROGER: Why not?

SHIRL: Haven't the foggiest.

ROGER: *(He hears a noise.)* What's that?

SHIRL: Sounds like your mother cleaning out the medicine chest.

ROGER: I thought—whoo! For a minute, I forgot. I almost thought it was Arlene. I thought she called my name.

SHIRL: That'll happen. You can count on the voices for six months, maybe a year. Scenes from the past, rolling out like a movie.

ROGER: All the way home from the hospital this morning she kept talking to me. Telling me where to turn, reminding me to pick up the shirts from the dry cleaner's.

SHIRL: No advice on your future?

ROGER: Not that I recall.

SHIRL: Voices always want you to live happily ever after.

ROGER: It was spooky.

SHIRL: Spooky is putting it mildly. My Mitchell had an opinion on everything. Mouthing off for years after he was dead.—I don't want to pressure you, but have you decided how long you want me?

ROGER: I can't think now. I can't decide anything.

Svetlana's New Flame

Olga Humphrey

Man & Woman

Svetlana (20's) a Russian émigré and Ted (20's) a side-show performer.

Scene: Coney Island and Brighton Beach

> *Here, two very different people encounter one another for the first time and sparks fly.*

O O O

Ted turns to Svetlana.

TED: Ma'am?

SVETLANA: Yes?

TED: Are you okay?

SVETLANA: Of course, of course. I have a job interview today. Does this look like a power suit to you? I was told in America the women have to wear a power suit to get a job.

TED: I think that'll do.

SVETLANA: And I have this briefcase, but it's empty. (She opens it and turns it upside down. Nothing comes out.) I didn't have anything to put in it.

TED: So you have an interview with Sid?

SVETLANA: Yes. You know him?

TED: I work for him.

SVETLANA: You work for Sid Wolff's Freak Show?

TED: I do.

SVETLANA: Oh.

TED: I'm Ted.

(He puts out his hand. She shakes it.)

SVETLANA: I am Svetlana.

TED: Are you sure you're all right?

SVETLANA: Why do you ask?

TED: Your face.

SVETLANA: Oh! It was a little accident. I'm learning to be a fire eater, I was practicing outside yesterday, and I guess it was too windy.

TED: *(To the audience.)* What an idiot.

SVETLANA: Excuse me?

TED: Nothing.

SVETLANA: What do you do for the Freak Show?

TED: I'm the Great Tedini.

SVETLANA: The Great Tedini. Ohhhh...And what is your specialty?

(Ted removes his hat. There are several nails sticking out of his head.)

TED: I'm also known as the Human Blockhead.

SVETLANA: You stick nails in your head?

TED: I don't just stick them in. I hammer.

SVETLANA: Oh. Doesn't that hurt?

TED: No more than eating fire.

SVETLANA: How did you come up with this?

TED: I always knew this is what I would do.

SVETLANA: Always?

TED: From the time I was a child, I would steal nails out of my father's tool box.

SVETLANA: And hammer them into your head?

TED: Well, back then, I was trying to hammer them into my brother's head. To this day, he still won't speak to me.

SVETLANA: It's a calling then?

TED: Yes, I guess you could say it is.

SVETLANA: Me, too.

TED: Why fire?

SVETLANA: I don't know. I was trying to figure out why the other day. Perhaps it has to do with coming to America. Being an émigré. Here, everything and everyone is like a light. All fired up, yes? The Empire State Building all different colors of light at night, like a beacon. New York in darkness from an airplane reminds me of diamonds. People on the street going so fast as if someone put a match under their behinds. Maybe, I too, want to shine brightly in my new home.

(A beat.)

TED: Well, good luck with the interview.

SVETLANA: Thank you, Ted.

Three Days of Rain

Richard Greenberg

Man & Woman
Ned (20's) an aspiring architect and Lina (20's) his roommate's girlfriend.

Scene: NYC, 1960

> *Ned and his roommate, Theo, will one day become world-famous architects. As struggling beginners, however, they meet the challenge of survival as true partners. A fight over a stolen design sends Theo away in a fit of anger. Here, Ned entertains Theo's girlfriend, Lina, and they discover a mutual attraction for one another.*

> *The rain continues. The light in the apartment is that cocoon-ish light you get sometimes on rainy afternoons, a muted array of the colors at the end of the spectrum. There's a fuss at the door.*

NED: *(Off-Stage.)* I'll—
LINA: Ooh—I'm shaking—it's—
NED: H-here's the key—
LINA: Wonderful! *(Key in the lock; they enter. Ned has a grocery bag.)* I'm going to drip all over your nice, dilapidated floor!
NED: Th-that's—Me, too.
LINA: That was gorgeous, wasn't it?
NED: Yes…G-give me your slicker. *(Lina takes it off.)* You're soaked through.
LINA: I don't mind. Oh, there aren't any warm fires here, are there? I forget—
NED: No—

LINA: Just banked ones—no, nothing.

NED: Y-you're going to catch cold or—

LINA: No, I don't. Isn't that moment thrilling, right before it starts, and everything turns purple and the awnings shake and the buildings ignite from the inside? I love that part.

NED: If you...n-need to change—

LINA: I don't mind just sopping for a while. But is there bourbon?

NED: I...No, I don't—

LINA: There must be—

NED: S-sorry—

LINA: I happen to know there is.

NED: ...There is?

(Lina goes to a box on top of a stack of books next to the drafting table, extracts bottle of Maker's Mark.)

LINA: Theo is not a big *sharer.*

NED: N-no.

LINA: Do you want some? *(Ned waves a hand, "I pass.")* You ought to, It makes everything *so* much better.

NED: Everything's...fine.

LINA: Is it?

NED: ...Today, yes. *(She sips drink she's made.)*

LINA: Yes. For me, too. It was funny running into you.

NED: Yes!

LINA: I didn't even realize I was here! I didn't even realize I'd come to this neighborhood. It was not my intention.

NED: What was?

LINA: I didn't have one.

NED: M-me, neither.

LINA: I was off from the bookstore, I just wandered away the day.

NED: Th-theo lift his robe.

LINA: ...U-u-u-h-h-h...well. Segue?

NED: I'm worried about you...in those things.

LINA: You are just desperate to get me out of my clothes, aren't you?

NED: I...don't want you to get sick.

LINA: ...Where's the robe?

NED: In the bathroom. On the hook.

LINA: I'll change. *(Crosses to bathroom.)* You can change in here when I do. I promise I won't look.

NED: I'm fine.

LINA: I promise I won't—

NED: I'm not as wet as you.

LINA: No, that's right, I'm *all* wet. Let me bring my drink. *(Passing him:)* I've seen this scene before, you know.
   (She goes into bathroom, keeps door open a crack. He starts unpacking bags onto counter, an array of vegetables, picked for color. From bathroom.) Hey!

NED: What?

LINA: Say something small to me while I'm changing!

NED: W-what?

LINA: Just chatter at me! I get restless!

NED: I...d-don't know what to say.

LINA: Just nonsense...palaver.

NED: Oh. *(Pause.)* D-do you believe in Original Sin?
   (Half-beat. She pokes her head around the door.)

LINA: *(As though answering his question.)* No, in fact, I don't believe I *have* seen any good movies lately, why have *you*?

NED: Oh...No.
   (Lina emerges in robe.)

LINA: Original Sin!

NED: I—

LINA: It's like tea-chat with Reinhold Niebuhr. Why. Do you?

NED: Um, yes, let's change the subject—

LINA: No, it's interesting to me—

NED: It's not—

LINA: It's just I've grown unaccustomed to the idea—

NED: It's peculiar—

LINA: With Theo, there are never any ghosts of any kind. Never any clouds or impediments. He's all sort of sharp and slender and gleaming—

NED: ...He's...

LINA: ...Rather a metallic young man...

126 men's and women's scenes

NED: He's... *(Pause.)*

LINA: *(Mostly to herself.)* But I swore I wouldn't do that today...
(Brightening deliberately:) What a beautiful harvest on that
countertop!

NED: I...liked the colors.

LINA: Are you going to just leave them there to look at? They'll
rot.

NED: No, I—

LINA: Or make dinner? I'm not *ang*ling.

NED: ...I thought I'd m-make dinner. *(Awkward moment.)*

LINA: I'll leave when the rain lets up a little.

NED: N-no—

LINA: Yes, I will—

NED: Your clothes have to dry—

LINA: I can wear them damp.

NED: ...All right. *(He gets a knife, starts chopping vegetables.)*
(With sudden gallantry:) Won't you please stay to dinner?

LINA: Give me that knife. *(He yields it. She starts chopping what
he was chopping. After a moment, she starts sniffing the air.)*
I've always rather *enjoyed* the smell of drenched wool on a
person.
*(He whips off his sweater. Lights. Rain louder. Half hour later.
They're finishing dinner.)*

LINA: That was spectacular!

NED: It was...just a salad.

LINA: No. It was like some fall-of-Rome variation on a salad. Every
leaf, every herb, every pepper-stick, it was Trimalchian.

NED: Th-thank you.

LINA: No—thank *you*... What time is it, do you know?

NED: The c-clock is broken. Early, though. M-maybe seven? If the
rain lets up, we can...s-see a movie later, if you like.

LINA: Yes, we could go out. What's playing?

NED: Mm...D-down the block, there's "The World of Suzie
Wong"—

LINA: Or we could stay in.

NED: Either way. Here. *(Pours her the last of the wine, hands it to her, smiles, about to say something.)*

LINA: What?

NED: Nothing…I'm…so happy; it's weird.

LINA: *(Puzzled by it.)* Yes! I know, me too!

NED: All day—

LINA: Yes, me too!…I usually wake in what they call a "brown study."—I have no idea what that means but I love to say it—"brown study"—but today…I got up and it wasn't raining yet but there was already the scent of it, and I had nothing at all to do. I made some coffee and lit a cigarette and read the dire newspaper and thought, well, all right, yes, give me another sixty years of this—

NED: I—Yes—

LINA: The two of us waking in a mood like that on the same morning—it's a statistical exorbitance! Given our natures.

NED: Yes—

LINA: We have to figure it out: What different thing did our days have in common? *(Pause. They look at each other; a sad recognition neither wants to say aloud.)*

NED: I'll clear the plates. *(He starts to.)*

LINA: Let me help you—

NED: No…I can.

LINA: …Okay. *(She sits, lights cigarette, while Ned cleans off dishes.)* Has he called you today?

NED: Y-yes.

LINA: Oh…And how is everything?

NED: He-he's…working v-very hard. Apparently, he's had, um, a brainstorm and—

LINA: Oh…good…

NED: Yes…He…s-says, he's f-finally onto…the real thing…he n-needed to get away and it's…c-come at last… When he comes b-back, we'll have to…p-play the March from "Scipio" or something…Hasn't he called you?

LINA: Yes. Well, I think so. I'm not sure.

NED: What?

LINA: Well, this morning, when I was reading the paper, the phone rang and rang for...ten minutes, I think. That was probably him.

NED: Oh...Would you like coffee?

LINA: I would dearly love some coffee. *(Ned starts to prepare some.)* Anyway, what did *you* do today?

NED: It was...nothing...the same as y-you—

LINA: Tell me anyway.

NED: I don't—

LINA: I'm getting that—feeling—just talk, talk...talk it away—

NED: ...What? Um...Okay... *(They look at each other.)* It was... same as you. I slept...late this morning and when I woke up, it was...already raining a little. And I felt so....light. Free, the way I n-never do. I went to the c-corner to buy coffee and a roll...and the pavement was slick and...jet in places and the sidewalk was this oily brown in places and...there were two woman in identical trench coats. One of them h-had just bought an African Violet plant and she kept tilting it so dirt kept falling on her...feet and...it s-surprised her each time so each t-time she would apologize to her...shoes, which I liked. I bought the coffee and sipped it and I...d-didn't come home right away. I walked out of my way because it was all so...pleasant, the day. I felt like a...flaneur.

LINA: What's a flaneur?

NED: Don't you know that word?

LINA: No. I don't know that word.

NED: A flaneur is a wanderer through the city. Someone, who... idles through the streets without a purpose...except to idle through the streets. And linger when it, when it...pleases him.

LINA: That's what he does?

NED: Yes.

LINA: What about work? Does he ever get to work?

NED: He has no work...if he's the real thing.

LINA: He just strolls?

NED: Yes. It's his career. He has a...pri-vate income.

LINA: Some vast sum—

NED: P-pennies but they...suffice. He d-doesn't need...much. Not what people need who have...intricate lives. He just...walks, you see. His life has no pattern...Just traffic...and no hope—

LINA: That's sad—

NED: Because he has no n-need of hope! The only thing he wants from life is...the day at hand. And when he's old...his memories aren't of Triumphs and Tragedies. He remembers...certain defunct cafes where he shared cups of coffee with...odd, scary strangers. And people he's known for years and years. Slightly.

LINA: Because it's a solitary thing to be a *flaneur*.

NED: Yes...but never lonely...I think.

LINA: Is that what you want to be?

NED: I haven't g-got the strength of character. But it's what I would w-wish...for someone better than I am. I think it would be the best thing! To be this...vagabond prince. Do you know? A wanderer through the city. A walker.

(Beat.)

LINA: Tell me about this house you two are making.

NED: No—

LINA: Theo never does—

NED: It's...idiotic

LINA: It isn't—it's exciting—it makes me want to—

NED: ...What?

LINA: —want to *be* something. I want to be...a painter!

NED: You do?

LINA: Or...a writer, a *belle—lettrist*!

NED: Oh—

LINA: Or a negro blues singer or just a very intriguing alcoholic...I am so terribly old.

NED: You're young—!

LINA: I'm a southern woman who admits to thirty—God alone knows what the truth of things must be—

NED: You're an in-infant—

130 men's and women's scenes

LINA: I'm *nothing.*

NED: You're—lovely—

LINA: *(On "lovely.")* Theo looks at me and sees...something from Anais Nin. Just because I'm gloomy, sometimes, and opaque, sometimes. And because when he picked me up, we were sketching naked men at the Art Students' League—these sorts of things impress him—he is so naive—he is so easily astonished—He sees me as one of those girls from fifteen years ago—all Quattrocento pale and dull-eyed and glazed and smugly silent because they possess the secret of the universe and you don't. *I* don't. That's what's funny—I am *never* silent—he must notice that—I smother the day in speech because I know nothing and I want someone to speak back to me and *tell* me—what? What is it that some people in cities seem to know? What is this secret that is constantly eluding me?

NED: *(Suddenly.)* There isn't any.

LINA: ...What?

NED: There isn't any s-secret. I used to...think that, too...but, no...no secret to be found...just...g-gestures...whims... energy...Personality, do you know?

LINA: *(Mordant, but serious.)* That's tragic.

NED: Is it? I thought...it was nice...when I realized. A relief.

LINA: And when was that?

NED: So recently.

LINA: Still...I want something... I suppose I'll marry Theo and that will be something—

NED: *(Abrupt.)* Is that happening?

LINA: Nobody ever says anything, but...what else? I'm so happy for you, that you have this house, that you're beginning something—

NED: I'm not...hap-py about—

LINA: But—

NED: It's going to...explode in our faces—

LINA: No—

NED: We're...we *are* too young, m-much too young, no one

has...ever d-done this so young—We should still be... hirelings...doing...restrooms and el-elevator shafts, but Theo—

LINA: Theo—

NED: He...*wants*. No one will ever commission us—

LINA: But this *house*—

NED: My p-parents. My parents. No indication at all—

LINA: But then you'll have this house and people will see it and come to you—

NED: *I-if* we have it; we're...waiting on Theo who's...waiting on God who's...blocked. Theo's been a little st-stalled since school and until he gets an idea that's real—

LINA: But you said he claims to have one—

NED: ...Y-yes. He does.

LINA: That makes you sad—

NED: No—

LINA: It does, though. Why does he have to have the idea?

NED: *(Slightly strict.)* Because that's how it is. Who knows what will come of this anyway? If I minded the prospect of cata-strophic failure, I never would have started the whole thing. ...This is what I imagine will happen:...My parents...will invest most of the money they have in this h-house...as a way of m-making up...and the house will never be built...or if it is b-built...it will collapse due to some mysterious and in-incalculable...design flaw. And we will all end up...dead. And bankrupt...strewn along...v-various gutters. I see this with...astonishing clarity. Bru-brutal clarity. Poverty. Hunger. Aban-bandonment. Incorporated. *(Beat.)* In my...darkest midnight hours, I...have this theory that... *(With one hand, he describes a column.)* Here are...our intentions...and here... *(With the other hand, a parallel column.)* is what actually happens...and the only thing spanning them *(He connects the two columns on top with an arc.)* is Guilt.

LINA: Guilt?

NED: The...preposterous instinct that we are...wholly re-respon-sible for events...completely out of our control. *(He makes the shapes again.)* What we want...what we get...guilt: It's an arch.

LINA: What you want... *(Lina does a line fairly low level.)* What you will get... *(She makes a parallel line at her full reach.)* Genius... *(A soaring line connecting the two.)* It's a...Flight path. An Ascent!

NED: *(Blushes, smiles.)* That's sentimental...Thank you. *(Beat.)*

LINA: You are such a nice man. This has been such a wonderful day! We have to...I want to...If only we really knew *how* to...

NED: What?

LINA: Cherish...this easy moment...when we mean so little to each other.
(Beat.)

NED: I think the coffee's ready.

LINA: ...Oh...oh, yes! *(Ned crosses to kitchenette.)* I think...the rain...The rain seems to have let up a little. Maybe I should...skip the coffee and take advantage of—

NED: Your clothes, though...They may not be...

LINA: Yes, but they may be—

NED: I'll check for you. *(He goes into bathroom, emerges a moment later. A little sadly)* Oh. They are.

LINA: Oh...I suppose I really ought to...

NED: All right. *(They smile, awkwardly, she crosses to bathroom, takes clothes off curtain-rod, mostly closed door.)* Lina.

LINA: *(Pokes head out.)* Yes?

NED: Oh. I just wanted to see...if I could...say your name...without fumbling it? And I did: L-l-l-lina.

LINA: Yes. You did.
(Hesitation. She goes back into bathroom.)
(Ned just stands there. Lina can be glimpsed, shaking dry her clothes. Ned starts to say something. Changes his mind. A moment. He speaks.)

NED: I'm always w-watching you. Whenever you're here...I can't help it. I try not to. Ev-ever since I met you. It's awful...I don't want it...I d-don't expect...to have things...like other people, but I'm...always th-thinking of you. It's h-horrible...I kn-know nothing can come of it...I know I can't have...the things I w-want. I shouldn't tell you this. I ca-can't stop, though. I'm sorry. I'm so sorry. You're s-so...fantastic, you're... D-don't let him t-take you down...the way he does. Don't let him...hurt you. You don't de-deserve it. You deserve only good things. N-not him. Not me. Or...I mean, not—

(By now, she has returned to the room. She looks at him.)

LINA: You're just...talking on and on—

NED: No—

LINA: You are.

NED: I don't waste words. I can't...afford to. *(A moment.)* I did-n't say anything—

LINA: But you did—

NED: F-forget it—

LINA: I don't want to. *(The rain is louder now.)* Look—it's started again! A downpour.

(Lights.)

Three the Hard Way

Linda Eisenstein

Man & Woman

Kathleen (30's) a fiery woman en route to her father's funeral, and Albert (58) her father; a ghost.

Scene: a pool hall in Northern California

> *When Albert dies in Reno, Kathleen travels there to meet her sisters at his funeral. When she stops at a pool hall for a rest, she and Albert, a pool player extraordinaire, play pool and shoot the breeze.*

○ ○ ○

> *At Rise: It is evening. In the dark, the loud sound or a power break on a pool table. As lights come up, Kathleen is playing pool in silence, using a custom cue, with surgical precision. Kathleen is deadpan; when she gets angry, her only change is to hit the ball harder.*

> *Albert appears, in a pool of light, holding his cue. During the scene, Kathleen mostly pays attention to her position on the table, rarely looking at Albert. He watches her play and kibitzes.*

> *(Note: Neither the pool game nor the pool table should be realistic. The table shimmers in light, the most important and magical place in the world. The actors use real cues and cue chalk but not real balls. All the emphasis should be on the actors' strokes and concentration. It should have the quality of an intense dream.)*

ALBERT: Nice shot. (*Kathleen reacts to his presence.*) Tough one.

KATHLEEN: I've been playing for shit these days.

ALBERT: I don't know why you go for the tough ones, though.

KATHLEEN: That's all there seems to be lately.

ALBERT: You always liked the tough shots. You're working too hard, Kathleen.

KATHLEEN: Tell me about it.

ALBERT: Listen to the old man. Go for the easy shots. You know the secret, don't you?

KATHLEEN: Yeah, yeah, I know.

ALBERT & KATHLEEN: Cue ball control.

ALBERT: That's right. Place the cue ball right and everything else comes naturally.

KATHLEEN: Easy for you to say.

ALBERT: Then the rest of it is easy as pie. Like shooting fish in a barrel.

KATHLEEN: I hated practicing that part. Cue ball control. I never had the patience for it.

ALBERT: Sure you do. You just like whacking 'em around. Making the pockets smoke with the fancy shots. The ones that made the boys too scared to come around.

KATHLEEN: Back off, Albert. I play the way I like. *(She misses a shot.)* Shit. *(She plays in silence for a moment or two.)*

ALBERT: So. Did you call Benny?

KATHLEEN: Benny. Jesus, Dad, you knew this. We're divorced.

ALBERT: I liked that boy.

KATHLEEN: Yeah, you sure did.

ALBERT: Now him, he wasn't afraid of you one bit.

KATHLEEN: Not nearly enough.

ALBERT: Whatever happened to him, anyway?

KATHLEEN: He moved to Florida.

ALBERT: No kidding, Miami?

KATHLEEN: Key West.

ALBERT: Boy sure could drink.

KATHLEEN: Yeah, he sure could.

ALBERT: Hell of a sax player, though. Beautiful tone. Best I've heard since Stan Getz.

KATHLEEN: Yeah, he was a player, all right.

ALBERT: Six in the corner.

   (Kathleen sinks the six.)

ALBERT: Ever think about getting back together with him?

KATHLEEN: No way, Dad.

ALBERT: You two try counseling? They say it helps.

KATHLEEN: It's a little late, Dad. It's been four years.

ALBERT: I never believed in it, either. Bunch of meddling fools. That's what fathers are supposed to say, though. "Get counseling. Stay together." Fuck it, do what you want, it's your life.

   (She plays for a moment or two in silence.)

ALBERT: Nice boy, though.

KATHLEEN: Yeah, he was.

ALBERT: Irreconcilable differences.

KATHLEEN: Yeah. I wanted to sleep with men and so did he. (A pause while she shoots.)

ALBERT: Good sax player, though.

KATHLEEN: Jesus, dad, do you mind?!

ALBERT: Sorry.

KATHLEEN: I mean, I'm trying to play over here.

ALBERT: Well, sink the four then.

KATHLEEN: (Looks at the table.) Why not the eight?

ALBERT: The four's the better shot.

   (Kathleen aims for the eight—and misses.)

KATHLEEN: Shit.

ALBERT: Stop trying so hard.

   (Kathleen steps back from the table, frustrated, while Albert demonstrates. She affects not watching.)

ALBERT: Let me show you something. (Albert picks up the cue ball and places it carefully.) Here: see that angle? That's the shot you're looking for. Not straight on, and not so oblique you have to shave it. That's the ideal angle.

KATHLEEN: The ideal angle.

ALBERT: Lookie here. (He shoots.) See how that breaks off the other one? It just strolls over into position. (He shoots again.)

men's and women's scenes 137

See? Shot after shot, the same easy walk. Play this way, you don't have to make those tough-guy shots. Just easy ones. One right after the other.

KATHLEEN: Sure, Dad.

ALBERT: It doesn't have to be hard all the time. It's okay for it to be easy.

KATHLEEN: What's the point then? Where's the challenge?

ALBERT: Challenge? You don't think this way is a challenge? Listen: Willie Mosconi played this way for eight and a half hours, ran 526 balls, and only had to stop because he got tired. You know the kind of concentration and control it takes, to get 'em to line up like that for you? Christ—try doing that in the rest of your life.

(Kathleen snatches up the cue ball, glares at him for a beat—then places it down. She begins to practice her cue ball control.)

ALBERT: Just trying to be helpful. Paternal. Give fatherly advice.

KATHLEEN: Right.

ALBERT: I know I don't quite have the hang of it. I never knew my own father, you know.

Kathleen. You've told me this before, Albert.

ALBERT: He died when I was four.

KATHLEEN: About a million times.

ALBERT: Consequently, I have no idea how a father is supposed to act.

KATHLEEN: No shit.

ALBERT: Much less with daughters. A complete mystery to me.

KATHLEEN: Boys would have been easier on you.

ALBERT: What makes you think that?

KATHLEEN: I don't know. I always assumed you wanted boys.

ALBERT: No. Hell no. What man in his right mind wants boys? Boys all hate their fathers. Read your Freud. Boys want to kill their fathers and screw their mothers. I never wanted boys. What in the world would make you think that?

KATHLEEN: You didn't exactly raise us like girls.

ALBERT: What's that supposed to mean?

138 men's and women's scenes

KATHLEEN: You didn't treat us like girls.

ALBERT: Like creampuffs, you mean? Like simpering morons, ready to keel over the minute someone says boo? Like Mary's friend, what's her name?

KATHLEEN: Patty's not a moron. She just acts…feminine.

ALBERT: Same thing.

KATHLEEN: Never mind. You wouldn't understand. You never did, Albert.

ALBERT: What's to understand?

KATHLEEN: For God's sake, Albert. For their eleventh birthdays, my friends all got Barbie. I got a cue case.

ALBERT: It was real leather.

KATHLEEN: It's not a joke, Dad. None of us ever had the faintest idea how to act like girls.

Albert. You're not girls—you're women.

KATHLEEN: The three of us? We're total freaks.

ALBERT: Most smart women are.

KATHLEEN: Mary—she doesn't even know how out of it she is. And Irene?

ALBERT: I regret my influence on Irene. Believe me.

KATHLEEN: She's even worse off than me. You really made a mess of us, Albert.

ALBERT: I was just trying to raise a family, the best way I knew how.

KATHLEEN: In a pool hall? Around gamblers and hustlers and pros? What kind of place is that for girls.

ALBERT: Actually, I thought of you three as people, not girls.

KATHLEEN: I don't fit in. I walk down the hall at work and people actually jump out of my way. I figured something out the other day: I never even learned how to smile right. Must have been all those hours sighting down a cue. I was watching these girls at the office. They do this…thing with their face. Animate it somehow. It has something to do with the eyes-blinking while you open them, maybe.

(She tries a feminine smile: raising her cheeks, while animating her face and widening and blinking her eyes.)

men's and women's scenes 139

ALBERT: Looks half-witted.

KATHLEEN: *(Continuing to smile this way.)* Men seem to like it. It's a lot of work, though. *(She drops it, becomes deadpan again.)* Gives me a headache.

ALBERT: Then don't do it.

KATHLEEN: I don't. That's my point. Most women have learned how to do this unconsciously. I have to work like a son-of-a-bitch, just to keep it up long enough to get through a lunch meeting. *(She "does" the smile again.)*

ALBERT: Looks painful.

KATHLEEN: *(Dropping the smile.)* I've been practicing, daily.

ALBERT: You'd be better off working on you cue ball control.

KATHLEEN: Yeah, well, we all know about your lifetime priorities. But I have a real job, thank you.

ALBERT: A likely story.

KATHLEEN: Hey—you know how much ad space I sold last month? $35,000.

ALBERT: Is that good?

KATHLEEN: For trade ads? In this economy? Hell, yes, it is. I beat everyone in the division.

ALBERT: This is face to face selling?

KATHLEEN: No, on the telephone.

ALBERT: Aha! There you go, then. I rest my case.

KATHLEEN: What case?

ALBERT: Do you smile on the phone, Kathleen? Make that half-witted little face while you're closing your sales?

KATHLEEN: No way.

ALBERT: I didn't think so. How do you do it, then?

KATHLEEN: You really want to know? It drives my co-workers crazy. As I talk? I do crossword puzzles.

ALBERT: See? Who says I didn't raise you right!

KATHLEEN: (Smiling.) Yeah.

ALBERT: The difference between a hustler and a pro. A hustler is always sweating it. A pro can afford to make it look easy.

KATHLEEN: Playing the ideal angle.

ALBERT: Just letting one bounce off the next one. One after the other.

KATHLEEN: I wish to God it was that easy. *(Pause.)* How come we never actually talked this way? I would have liked a normal conversation now and again.

ALBERT: Well, we'll have one now.

KATHLEEN: Oh sure. Fat lot of good it does now.

(An awkward silence.)

ALBERT: Let's see. So. How's life going for you, Kath?

KATHLEEN: At the moment? What do you think? Love life nil. Wrestling with the J.O.B. Trying to get my bank account back up past ground zero, after Irene's last escapade.

ALBERT: How much she hit you up for?

KATHLEEN: None of your business. *(Softening a little.)* Sorry. I'm still feeling a little burned.

ALBERT: Tell me about it.

KATHLEEN: You too? That's funny. Somehow it never occurred to me that she'd come to you for money.

(Albert shrugs.)

KATHLEEN: Why did you give her money?

ALBERT: Why did you?

(They're both silent.)

ALBERT: Maybe the same reasons, then.

KATHLEEN: No, not the same. Definitely not.

ALBERT: Probably not then. I give it to her because deep down, she's just like me. You give it to her to prove that deep down, she's nothing like you.

(Kathleen begins unscrewing her cue, putting it away.)

KATHLEEN: This is not working.

ALBERT: Ah, the end of the game.

KATHLEEN: Unfortunately, it's just beginning. *(Rubs her eyes.)* Jesus, I'm tired. And I still have hours more to drive.

ALBERT: When you're on the road and tired of driving, stop and find a pool hall. Best pit stop in the world.

KATHLEEN: I hate Reno. Why did you have to die in Reno?

ALBERT: *(After a beat.)* Funerals are a pain in the ass. I always avoided them, myself. Wakes are better, actually. At least there are things to eat and drink. I appreciate you making the trip.

KATHLEEN: Someone has to clean up your mess. I have to get going. Mary's probably been there for hours, worrying her head off. I wonder if she ever reached Irene.

ALBERT: You three have to hang together now, Kath.

KATHLEEN: Easier said than done.

ALBERT: Just don't try to do it the hard way. Take the easy shots. One at a time.

(Albert moves out of light.)

KATHLEEN: It's funny. I check the corners of every pool hall I walk into. I always half-expect to find you there. Even now. Jesus. Maybe I always will. You think so, Albert? *(She turns, looks for Albert.)* Albert? *(He's gone.)* Daddy? *(She clicks her case closed.)* Goddamn it. Why aren't you here. You're supposed to be here.

(Blackout)

An Unhappy Woman

Michael T. Folie

Man & Woman
Gayle (30-40) an unhappy woman, and Hank (30-40) a happy man.

Scene: here & now

> When Gayle and Hank meet on a train platform, all kinds of sparks fly.

○ ○ ○

> At rise: Hank and Gayle wait on a commuter platform. We know this because a sign says 'Commuter Platform, Track 4.' Both are dressed in business attire. He reads a newspaper. She watches him, becoming more and more uncomfortable. He turns a page of the newspaper, loudly snapping out the creases. Gayle can't take it anymore. (Note: Parentheses indicate where dialogue is overlapped by the next line.)

GAYLE: Hey! You wanna get shot?! Hey! I'm talking (to you!)

HANK: Are you (speaking to me. Miss?)

GAYLE: Because you keep reading the paper like that. I guarantee you, somebody on this platform's gonna pull out a piece and blow you (the fuck away.)

HANK: For reading (the paper?)

GAYLE: And it might be me. It's the *way* you read the paper. Snapping it around like you were sitting on the john in some (private men's club.)

HANK: I'm sorry if it (bothers you.)

GAYLE: You know what that sounds like, when you snap the paper like that? Huh?

HANK: No. What?

GAYLE: Like a nine-millimeter Glock. Pocka! Pocka! Pocka! You can't make a noise like that in a public place!

HANK: I can't?

GAYLE: You gotta fold the paper into nice, tight, little quiet sections. You! You're all over the place with it. It's sloppy. It's sloppy commuting. Give me that!

(She snatches the newspaper. During the following, she folds the paper into thin sections.)

HANK: I didn't know there were such high standards for commuting.

GAYLE: There are high standards for life, Mister! Why do you think everything's so fucked up? 'Cause' of idiots like you. Inter-active fields of chaos bungling through life like big sloppy balls of dirty spaghetti. *(Pause.)* Where the hell you from anyway?

HANK: Washington.

GAYLE: The state? Or the cesspool?

HANK: Washington ,D.C.

GAYLE: Ah. An inside-the-Beltway kinda guy, huh?

HANK: Does it show?

GAYLE: You don't know how to act in the real world, buddy, that's what shows. *(She gives him back paper.)* Here! I just saved your life. Now go stand somewhere else. Somebody shoots your ass, I don't wanna get blood and stuff all over my new suit.

(Pause. Neither move.)

HANK: Excuse me, but...are you married or...living with someone?

GAYLE: What do you think?

HANK: I can't imagine you are.

GAYLE: *(High pitched mimicry.)* 'I can't imagine you are.' Why don't you talk like a man?

HANK: Your standards seem pretty high. Can anyone meet them?

GAYLE: Not you, that's for sure.

HANK: What's your name?

GAYLE: Who wants to know?

HANK: Hank.

GAYLE: *(Trying it on.)* Hank. *(Pause, expelling air sharply with the word.)* Hank. *(Pause, very nasal.)* Hannnnnk. *(Pause.)* Nope. Doesn't work for me. Henk.

HANK: What's your name?

GAYLE: Maybe it's Gayle. Hunk.

HANK: Can I ask you a question. Maybe—It's—Gayle?

GAYLE: Whataya think you been doing?

HANK: Are you ever…happy?

GAYLE: Happy?

HANK: You seem pretty unhappy to me.

GAYLE: Of course I'm unhappy! Everybody's unhappy!

HANK: (Not everybody.)

GAYLE: *(Going right on over him.)* Life sucks! Oh?! Who's happy?! The world is a giant food processor that just grinds people into tiny little bits. And this giant food processor of life, it's only got two speeds: boring, and terrifying!

HANK: Go on. What else? *(During the following, Hank pulls out a notebook and begins to write in it as Gayle speaks.)*

GAYLE: I gotta risk my neck every day to get to some stupid job I hate, just so I can afford to have a bar code and live in a god-damn Security Zone. Work sucks. Home is boring. And the trip between the two is a nightmare, filled with idiots like you snapping the fucking paper around. What are you doing, writing this all down in your little notebook?

HANK: And you don't know anyone whom you would describe as 'happy?'

GAYLE: What are you selling?

HANK: Because it is my experience that opposites attract. Maybe —It's—Gayle. Very unhappy people like yourself tend to attract very happy people.

GAYLE: And you're looking for some very happy people?

HANK: That I am.

GAYLE: Uh-huh. See you around. Hynk.

(She starts to go.)

Hank. Wait! Don't go. I could, uh, I could use a little help.

GAYLE: You could use a lot of help. So what?

HANK: Help. Getting along. Outside the Beltway. You know. You could...you could give me a few lessons.

GAYLE: No way! Not if you paid me in Yen!

HANK: You wouldn't, by any chance, be free for dinner tonight?

GAYLE: What time?

HANK: How about I pick you up at six-thirty?

GAYLE: How about I pick you up at six. And don't bother getting dressed. I'll pick out your clothes when I get there. Now lemme see your gun.

(Hank pulls out a large automatic pistol. She examines it, impressed.)

GAYLE: Oooh! A big one. I suppose you wanna see mine.

(She rummages around in her purse. He lays a hand on hers, stopping her.)

HANK: I'd rather save that for our wedding night.

GAYLE: You're old fashioned. I like that.

We Make A Wall

Gary Garrison

Man & Woman
Angie (35) a woman trying to restart her life, and Daniel (17) her son.

Scene: Bensonhurst, Brooklyn

> *After seventeen years, Angie has left her husband and son. Six months after her dramatic and unexplained departure, she returns to finally confront the two men she felt she had to leave. Here, she is greeted at the door by Daniel, who is obviously overjoyed to see his mom again.*

ANGIE: Daniel, tell your father he's got two minutes and I'm outta here! Two minutes, I got a life now, and I wantta live some of it. Ya' got that?

DANNY: *(Off-stage.)* Got it, ma!

ANGIE: *(Turning in.)* Jesus, Angie, what the hell are you doing here? Like you got nothin' better to do than to hear that guido make his excuses. God, give me the patience to accept the things I cannot stand and…

(Danny bursts in the room, all smiles and a big hug for his mother.)

DANNY: Ma, look at you! Wow! Turn around… WOW! Ya' look great. You got an ass on you, ma. Did ya' know that? D'ya bring the sauce?

ANGIE: What do you think? Would your mother not make the sauce you asked her to make one hundred times on the phone yesterday? And don't look at your mother's ass, Danny. There is no support for that in the Catholic church. Sauce is right there.

(Angie points to a large paper bag sitting on the floor beside the chair.)

DANNY: And the meatballs?

ANGIE: Thirty five.

DANNY: Thirty-five?! Ma, that's nothin'. That'll be gone before lunch.

ANGIE: So you tell father to keep his fat hands outta your bag, alright? Those are *your* meatballs, Danny. Not your father's. Your father gets gotz.

DANNY: Yeah. Right. Like I could keep him from your meatballs. Just the mention of your name and…

ANGIE: What is wrong with you, Danny? Your still lettin' your father push you around? I am twice your age and half your height, and I'm not afraid of him. Learn from the little people, Danny.

DANNY: Yeah, right.

(Angie crosses to the folding chair, sits.)

ANGIE: So how's Marla?

DANNY: Marla?! Forget her, ma. She's buggin'. She's like, mad-whacked.

ANGIE: *(A beat, then.)* I'm suppose to know what that means?

DANNY: Buggin', ma. She's…she's like tryin' to play me, but I'm up on it. So you know, I got my own strats.

ANGIE: Danny, what the hell are you talking about? Are you seeing her or not? And stop with the Snoopy Doggy Do.

DANNY: Doggy-*Dog*, ma. His name is Snoop Doggy-*Dog*.

ANGIE: Daniel, I do not care if his name is My Big Ass, talk to me so I can understand you. Now, are you seeing Marla or not?

DANNY: Not. Ever. Okay, maybe for the prom, 'cause she already got the dress and all. But after that, no. And you know what I discovered, ma? She snores. Swear to God. I'm at her house, right? We're watching like Nightmare on Elm Street, Part Whatever, and she falls asleep with her head right on my shoulder. I'm thinkin' this is nice. I'm thinkin' this like, you know, a Kodak moment or some shit. And then, THEN, she starts with the snore. I swear to God I thought it was like a joke, or something. And I'm laughing. And she's snoring, like… *(Exaggerated snore.)* …and I'm almost peeing in my pant's 'cause I'm thinking, damn, how can that kinda noise come out that little hole? But I think she's joking, right? So I say, "Marla? MARLA!" But it ain't no joke, ma. She's so asleep that I coulda had my way with her and she would have never known it. But she didn't have to worry, 'cause I wasn't going near that buzz saw. So now what?

ANGIE: What do you mean, so now what? You love her, that's what. And like she was gold, Danny, 'cause she is, and 'cause she loves you. And 'cause she ain't never told you HER laundry list of things YOU do that make her crazy.

DANNY: You're wrong, ma. She has.

ANGIE: She's got her nerve. What the hell did she say about you? Don't answer that. Never mind. In spite of whatever, she loves you anyway. That's what women do…until they can't do it no longer.

DANNY: *(Looking around at the empty room.)* Is that when they empty out the house and leave?

ANGIE: Sooner, if they're smart. I wasn't so smart.

DANNY: No, but you were quick. I can't believe you emptied out this house—from top to friggin' bottom in two days. You shoulda seen the look on dad's face when he came in here after you emptied everything out. Jesus Mercy Christ the Lord, ma. I thought he was going to stroke out or something. Swear to God, the veins were bulging in his forehead. Look like a friggin' special effect—you know, Spielberg, or something. Scared the hell out of me.

ANGIE: Don't be afraid of your father, Danny. That's no good. Respect, yes. Honor, yes…

DANNY: *(Interrupting.)* I'm not afraid of him, I just can't leave him like you did. I got no where to go. Uncle V says if I leave, I can't stay with him 'cause there's already bad blood between he and dad. And I can't go with you 'cause I don't know why, 'cause you never explained it, but dad says you say I can't. *(A beat, then.)* Is that right, me? I can't stay with you? *(A beat, then.)* Goddamn it! Answer me, ma!

ANGIE: WHERE DID YOU GET THAT MOUTH? You want to kiss

your mother with that same mouth? No! I don't think so! And don't you curse at me, young man, I did not raise you to curse at people, especially the one woman who has cried a river, A RIVER, of tears for you. No, not her! Do not curse at her. Understand me, Daniel?

DANNY: *(Quietly.)* Sorry, ma', I just...you know, I don't know what to do with all these feelings I got. So they come outta me at a lotta the wrong times. You know that guidance counselor at school, Miss James, you know the one with that big, red birthmark on her lip, she says I'm "raw." That what she says. "Danny, you're raw." Every time she sees me in the hall she gets choked up, like she knows something I don't. Like she can see five years down the road that I'm gonna kill myself or worse.

ANGIE: What's worse than killing yourself?

DANNY: I don't know. Staying here for longer than I have to would be pretty bad.

(Angie crosses to her son, takes his hands in hers and looks deep in his eyes.)

ANGIE: Danny...sweetheart...son...you wouldn't do anything like that, would you, Danny? You know, hurt yourself, or... you know.

DANNY: No. What for?

ANGIE: Sure you are. You're my boy, aren't you?

DANNY: *(Brightening.)* Yeah. That's right, ma. I am. And I'm going to do good by you. You'll see.

ANGIE: Of course you will, baby. Now you call your ma anytime...

DANNY: Yeah?

ANGIE: ...for meatballs.

DANNY: Or maybe sometimes, you know...just to talk.

(A long beat. Angie studies Danny's face.)

DANNY: What are you lookin' at, ma? Jeez, you makin' me feel all weird and stuff.

ANGIE: You look good, Danny...and you call me any time, sweetheart. Now get your father before I leave and stay gone another six months.

WOMEN'S SCENES

The Audition, or Guilty in a Court of Love

Jeff Goode

2 Women

Inger (20's) an auditioning actress and Jen (20's) her roommate, yet another auditioning actress.

Scene: an audition space

> *As you all know, the perfect monologue is a rare find. Here, roommates clash over a monologue at an audition.*

○ ○ ○

Enter Inger to audition.

INGER: Hello, my name is Inger Hatlen. My first audition piece will be the part of April from *Guilty in a Court of Love*. *(She begins.)* I took the fifth because I was protecting you. I lied to everyone because I didn't want to incriminate you...

JEN: You bitch! *(Jen has entered, livid. Inger, completely taken aback, turns to look at her.)* That's my audition piece. You stole it from me.

INGER: *(Bewildered.)* What the hell are you doing?

JEN: You knew I was doing April from *Guilty in a Court of Love*.

INGER: I did not.

JEN: Where did you find it?

INGER: It was on the kitchen table.

JEN: That was my copy!

INGER: So? I didn't know you were going to audition with it.

JEN: You should have asked me.

INGER: *You* didn't ask *me*.

JEN: I didn't think you were going to steal my monologue.

INGER: *(Aside to auditors.)* Can I start over? *(Jen grabs her arm.*

Inger jerks it away and turns on Jen, still trying not to make a scene, but getting very angry now.) I saw the script on the kitchen table, you weren't around, so I read it, and I picked this monologue to do, but I didn't steal it from you, and if you want to do it, too, fine, go ahead, do it, it's a free country.

JEN: My audition is right after yours! I can't do the same monologue right after you!

INGER: Too bad.

JEN: You did this on purpose! I asked you to call in and sign me up for an audition time and you signed up for the slot right before me because you knew we were doing the same piece.

INGER: *(Dryly, to the auditors.)* This is my roommate, Jen. She's a wacko. I should probably have her committed, but we need the eggs.

JEN: *(Also aside to the auditors.)* All right, can I just say one thing? I'm looking for monologues for this audition, and my friend Dawn in New York sends me this script *which is not available in this area*, because there's this great monologue in it. And I decide to do it because not only is it a great monologue, but probably *nobody* has heard it before, and I leave it on the kitchen table for maybe one day, and my roommate steals it.

	INGER:
And not only does she plan to audition with the same piece, but she volunteers to call in and sign us up for an audition time so she can arrange for her to go first, and shouldn't there be some kind of rule about this?	I did not. I did not. I did not. Bullshitbullshitbullshit bullshitbullshit.

INGER: *(To auditors.)* I did not know— *(Decides to tell Jen instead.)* I did not know you were going to audition with this monologue.

JEN: You heard me rehearsing every night this week.

INGER: Now, you think I was listening at the door, I suppose. I don't know what you're rehearsing in your room.

JEN: The walls are paper thin! I know you can hear every word I say.

INGER: They're not that thin.

JEN: Oh yeah? Then where did I hear this: "Uh uh. Ja—Ja—Ja—Ja—Ja—Jamallll!!!" Jamal jamal jamal jamal jamal..." *(Inger is flabbergasted.)* Was that some sort of celestial vision I was having??

(Inger turns to the auditors, ashen, while Jen launches into the monologue.)

INGER: I was not expecting any special favors.

If Jamal wants to cast me, I hope it's because I'm right for the role, and not because...	JEN: I took the fifth because I was protecting you. I lied to every one because I didn't want to incriminate you. And I lied to you
Well, not because of other things that it might be if there...	because I didn't want you to know that you *weren't* manipulating me. Every time you thought you tricked me or
(With resolve now:)	betrayed me, I betrayed myself. I let you use me. I forced you to use me. And now how do you feel?
were other things, which there aren't because nothing happened, because I'm not that kind of person, and I would never do that, and if you can't see that, THEN FUCK YOU ALL! *(Charging at Jen:)* That's my monologue	*(Continue until attacked.)* You feel guilty. You could have laughed all the way to my electric chair if you thought you were taking advantage of an innocent little girl. But now there's something warped about the whole thing. It makes your skin crawl, doesn't it?

JEN: Help!! Help! Time! Time! Somebody call time!

(Inger tries to strangle Jen, but Jen comes out on top and

strangles Inger. Continue until someone calls "time" or Inger is dead.)

The Beekeepers
C. J. Critt

2 Women
Patty (30's) a divorcee and Ginger (30's) her married friend.

Scene: a cafe table at Borders Books

Here, two good friends kibbitz over latte.

O   O   O

Lights up on the women at the book store.

PATTY: One more sip of mocha latte jave and I'm going to spew!
GINGER: Oh really?
PATTY: Either that or sprout hair on my palms and levitate.
GINGER: That'll make a hell of an entry in the Borders' cafe
    newsletter.
PATTY: Do you want to wait for that book signing?
GINGER: Naw.
PATTY: Oh.
GINGER: Well, I thought I did, but I don't.
PATTY: Good. I loaned my copy to my jazzercize car pool partner
    and I really didn't want to have to buy another one.
GINGER: There's only so much rock star autobiography a person
    can take, anyway.
PATTY: Especially when they're written by the ex-wives and girl-
    friends. I mean, isn't a lifetime backstage pass and a pile of
    palimony enough for them?
GINGER: Apparently not. *(Applies lipstick.)*
PATTY: "Wah!—He left his sequin jacket on the floor. Wah!
    Groupies for breakfast. Complain, complain, yada yada, give
    me the three million clams. What a crock!
    (Ginger spritzes with Binaca then hands it to Patty.)

GINGER: I had a dream about that guy in my office.

PATTY: The Brad Pitt clone.

GINGER: The same.

PATTY: Wow. Good?

GINGER: Oh yes.

PATTY: Did you do it?

GINGER: Absolutely.

PATTY: In the dream?

GINGER: No, in front of the water cooler during the fire drill.

PATTY: Ginger, are you mocking me?

GINGER: Patty, please. Of course it was during the dream, what do you think, he looks like Brad Pitt, for Christ sakes.

PATTY: Can you believe what those girls did?

GINGER: What? What girls?

PATTY: You know. The ones in *Thelma and Louise*. Killing themselves after having sex with Brad Pitt.

GINGER: It's only a movie.

PATTY: I know. But that just ruined it for me. My God, wouldn't you want to live. And tell everyone.

GINGER: I would…

PATTY: Going over a cliff in a convertible. Some ending. I hated it.

GINGER: It was kinda tragically stupid.

PATTY: Yeah, like walking in front of a train.

GINGER: And impulsive.

PATTY: Or taking heroin.

GINGER: Or snake handling.

PATTY: Or playing Russian roulette.

GINGER: Yeah… *(Pause.)* Wanna go dancing?

PATTY: Yeah!

(Lights blackout.)

Death Club—Ladies Auxiliary

Stephanie Griffin

2 Women

Lucy (70's) a widow comfortable with death and Gertrude (70's) her friend.

Scene: a funeral parlour

Here, two old friends share insight while visiting a deceased acquaintance at the funeral home.

○ ○ ○

Into the same funeral parlor viewing room walk, Gertrude and Lucy. They walk to the powder blue casket. They make the sign of the cross, and kneel, as in prayer over the body of a woman their age. A wreath of flowers with a ribbon strip which reads, 'Beloved Lena Genetti' covers the casket. They whisper.

GERTRUDE: It's a shame.
LUCY: God works in funny ways.
GERTRUDE: She's beautiful.
LUCY: I hated her.
GERTRUDE: Why?
LUCY: Because she was beautiful.
GERTRUDE: You hardly knew her.
LUCY: She's still beautiful.
GERTRUDE: She's dead.
LUCY: I still hate her.
GERTRUDE: The woman is dead.
LUCY: I don't hate her because she's dead. I hate her because she is beautiful.

GERTRUDE: She looks sixty-five. She had to be eighty if she's a day, how do you account for it?

LUCY: Only the good die young.

GERTRUDE: Lucy!

LUCY: I hate self-confident people. I've always hated self confident people. So smug. Life goes their way all the time kind of people.

GERTRUDE: Ah look at her, she's dead.

LUCY: No, I can't look at her. I can't look at her. She's dead, I know that, I still can't look at her. To tell the truth, she drove me crazy. For the most part, that wouldn't bother me, I mean someone's dead, live and let live, but with her, she just drives me crazy. I couldn't look at her, I couldn't listen to her talk. You know how some people make you feel like you have done everything wrong? It's in the way they talk, their tone, they always seem to have done the right thing and you have done the wrong? That's how it was with her. That's just how it was with her. It's like we are in some kind of sick race, and I lose. No matter how you cut it, I lose, it's like, if I was playing with this deck of cards in Atlantic City, I'd stay home.

GERTRUDE: Ah, she was a little strange, but…I'm gonna miss her, even though she was a pain in the ass. But you know, I saw baby pictures of her, she never smiled, not even then. You know some people, some people are born sad, born unhappy. It's just how they are. They can't change their nature. We start off the same and we end the same.

LUCY: Except you have clothes when you leave.

GERTRUDE: Well, what will be will be. She's gone.

LUCY: Whatever it was, I can't look at her now. It will make me crazy—probably make her crazy too.

GERTRUDE: She looks beautiful. Oh, she looks beautiful. I don't know who picked out her dress, but she looks beautiful. Even this casket, beautiful. Well, you know her husband, God rest his soul, he worked for the city…

LUCY: Oh yeah. What kind of work did he do?

GERTRUDE: I wonder who picked out her dress?

160 women's scenes

LUCY: When I die, pick out something nice for me.

GERTRUDE: You pick it out.

LUCY: It's bad luck.

GERTRUDE: You want people going through your things after you're gone?

LUCY: I can't choose between vanilla or chocolate, you think I can choose a dress to wear?

GERTRUDE: Let's pick it out now.

LUCY: Now? I don't know when I'm gonna die.

GERTRUDE: These things always happen in three's.

LUCY: I have the dress from Tommy's wedding. I gave away the dress from Pete's wedding, but the one from Tommy's wedding…Lena took me to get it. Blue, nice dress.

GERTRUDE: We could put it in one of those plastic clothes bags; the shoes, underwear, all together. What about your glasses?

LUCY: I'm not so interested in seeing everything clearly. I like things a little fuzzy now. I won't need 'em. Where I'm goin, the good Lord will provide.

GERTRUDE: How do you want to wear your hair? Up or down?

LUCY: I was gonna be a beautician.

GERTRUDE: Oh yeah?

LUCY: My mother put the deposit down and everything. Fifty dollars. Then my father died, so I had to quit school. I always said I'd go back. Yeah, then everyday I did nothing, now I'm here.

GERTRUDE: *(Touching Lucy's hair.)* Time flies. I like this fluff you have…but we're talking about a big day, people coming and looking, your last chance, like your wedding, it's your big day…

LUCY: You know these things wear me out. They take something out of me. You know everybody goin'…these get smaller…I worry, who's gonna come to mine?

GERTRUDE: I'll come.

LUCY: Promise?

GERTRUDE: I promise.

LUCY: Ah, get out of here. How can you promise? Huh? Huh? How can you promise?

(She starts trying to get a spot out of the satin lining in the coffin.)

GERTRUDE: Lena'd be mortified. She'd die if she saw this. You could eat off her floors.

(Lucy joins her.)

LUCY: Whatever Lena was, she was clean. You won't let them have people see me in filth like this? Would you? Promise me you'll clean it up.

GERTRUDE: You know, she'd carry a jar of Spic & Span in her bag—in case you know, germs on the cards. Could use it now.

LUCY: What cards?

GERTRUDE: Bingo.

LUCY: I'd go with you.

GERTRUDE: Where?

LUCY: To Bingo.

GERTRUDE: I always went when she went.

LUCY: You never ask me.

GERTRUDE: I hate bingo. I only did it to satisfy Lena. I never won. Bingo everyday, everywhere. Bingo today at Saint Frances; Monday night at Saint Ann's; Thursday afternoon...ah, she always stopped on the way to bingo to play the numbers. She always played three-eleven-seventy-seven. Day her mother died. Isn't it funny how things work out. She didn't want to play last week. She had the number but she didn't play it. A buck and a half—she would have gotten $368.00.

LUCY: That much? I didn't know that.

GERTRUDE: Five hundred on the dollar. Like the bookies. My mother would have been 109. She's dead twenty-five years, twenty-sixth of May. She died near Mother's Day.

LUCY: My mother would have been 101 on May thirteenth. I played that number with the bookie—never hit it.

GERTRUDE: You will one day, one day.

LUCY: My husband, Nino, he's been gone twenty years in August. The twelfth. *(Blesses herself.)*

GERTRUDE: God rest his soul.

LUCY: Ah, you can't change people. He was a son of a gun, hey what are you gonna do? You let the chips fall as they may.

GERTRUDE: Watch what you say about the dead.

LUCY: On our wedding night. I waited and waited, he forgot, went home to his mother.

GERTRUDE: No!

LUCY: He was a drunk.

GERTRUDE: He was your cross…

LUCY: I stayed with him. We never went out, but when we did I always left with him. I just did. I was mortified. Maybe that's why I'm backward socially. All those years…

GERTRUDE: Oh, everyone drank, it was the war.

LUCY: One time, I gave him his ring back and he cried on the street corner. Mrs. Petrulli came and told mama. She felt sorry for him and told me to take the ring back. He was drunk.

GERTRUDE: God was good to me. Sammy was a drunk, but he was fun, then he got the diabetes. Couldn't touch a drop.

LUCY: You were lucky. Stopped the booze before he got nasty.

GERTRUDE: Yeah, I know. He didn't drink, but he could get a little testy. Food was medicine with that diabetes, he always had to have food. Food was medicine, always had to have an orange or an apple, he was like a baby like that, pain in the neck. Past is the past…

LUCY: Mama said it was my own fault. I waited too long he was all I could get. He used to say, count no man lucky before he's dead. I put it on his gravestone.

GERTRUDE: After Sammy died, I cook when I want, I eat when I want. I try to remember the good times.

LUCY: I feel like my whole life stopped counting when he died. Do you ever think who you might bring on Noah's ark? Actually, who you might kick off of Noah's ark. Just stand there at the gang plank. *(As if two voices going back and forth.)* "You, unfortunately have never been very nice to me. Every opportunity you have had you have made life hard for me." "Oh, no he's my friend." "He's no friend of mine." "Are you asking me to choose between you and him?" "I'm just telling you he's not coming on my boat."

GERTRUDE: Lucy!

LUCY: Yeah, it's evil. I don't care. Makes me feel good. You know, I've been thinking. How long have we been coming to these funerals?

GERTRUDE: Paying our respects?

LUCY: Yeah.

GERTRUDE: After Netty's sister-in-law died. She was somethin' else. Do you remember her? Remember it was her daughter-in-law who was trying and trying to get pregnant and then on the feast of St. Ann's and it happened. I said today is the day.

A Garden of Women

Ludmilla Bollow

2 women

Mary Coletta and Mary Theresa (both in their 20's), novices in the order.

Scene: the garden of the Wyndham Estate, now a cloister, 1925

Mary Theresa has agonized over whether on not to make the final commitment to the order and here delivers her decision to her friend, Mary Coletta.

○ ○ ○

MARY THERESA: Wait. Mary Coletta?

MARY COLETTA: What is it, Mary Theresa?

MARY THERESA: Come, sit for a minute.

MARY COLETTA: Yes, for a moment. *(They sit. Pause.)* This is such a lovely garden, always overflowing with the presence of God.

MARY THERESA: Especially today, honoring His mother, crowning her Queen of the May.

MARY COLETTA: I didn't know, had no idea, what it would be like here. The other convents I visited, when I was younger— their cells were dark and dingy. I almost changed my mind about becoming a nun, but not for long.

MARY THERESA: I so wanted to join this order, it didn't matter where they were cloistered.

MARY COLETTA: Out here, I never feel cloistered, as if there's no separation between heaven and earth.

MARY THERESA: How miraculous, that the motherhouse came to own such a magnificent property.

MARY COLETTA: God works in mysterious ways. I believe that more and more.

MARY THERESA: So do I.

MARY COLETTA: It was His hand that helped write the will. Why else would a widow, who wasn't even Catholic, leave her entire estate to our Catholic order?

MARY THERESA: Why else?

MARY COLETTA: The order almost turned it down, claiming the Wyndham estate was too pretentious a place for an austere convent.

MARY THERESA: Pretentious? It looks like it was just waiting to be a convent—already fenced—gated. The stained glass solarium makes a beautiful chapel.

MARY COLETTA: Why would ordinary people want to fence themselves in? They have no need to shut out the world.

MARY THERESA: Shutting out the world—that would be the most difficult sacrifice—when taking the vows. Never to see my family again.

MARY COLETTA: They let you leave, if immediate family dies.

MARY THERESA: I don't want to see them when they're dead.

MARY COLETTA: But it's the sacrifices that purifies us.

(Mary Veronica and Mary Bernadette leave the garden.)

MARY THERESA: I know. And it is so easy to remain pure, here, away from the wickedness of the world. Yet, sometimes, on my pallet at night—when my body writhes—I can't keep dear Timothy from my thoughts.

MARY COLETTA: You must banish such temptations, immediately, harshly.

MARY THERESA: I do! I pray—I cry out to all the saints.

MARY COLETTA: When I miss my family at night, I come out here. Pray the rosary, contemplate the Joyful Mysteries. Seeing the stars—the heavens, I'm closer to God, and everyone else. Connected to all things—and the ache for family is subdued.

MARY THERESA: I miss—I—I need to talk to someone.

MARY COLETTA: Sister Ursula urges us to come to her, anytime there are doubts. She said we would have so many at first, and if prayer didn't dissolve them, we should openly discuss what is troubling us with her—before, not after, our vows.

MARY THERESA: I cannot talk about this with Sister Ursula.

MARY COLETTA: Do not choose me. I am only a simple novice.

MARY THERESA: I must tell someone. I need this confession.

MARY COLETTA: Pray.

MARY THERESA: I have. Endlessly.

MARY COLETTA: I will pray with you.

MARY THERESA: No—I just need you to listen.

MARY COLETTA: I will listen today. But once we take our vows, we must observe the rules of silence.

MARY THERESA: *(Looking away, clenching hands in prayer.)* I am not taking the vows.

MARY COLETTA: What! Why, Mary Theresa? Why, after all these years of preparation?

MARY THERESA: *(Begins walking in circle.)* I'm not sure how to reveal this, but I must.

MARY COLETTA: Do not be so troubled, Mary Theresa. Sit. I will listen.

MARY THERESA: *(Sits.)* This is what I must tell you, and only you… One night, I came out here, and I knelt by that huge rock to pray. I heard this sound—coming from deep within the earth.

MARY COLETTA: What kind of sound?

MARY THERESA: A child, crying, calling out to me—

MARY COLETTA: A child?

MARY THERESA: Yes. "Mama—mama—," the voice kept calling, over and over.

MARY COLETTA: Have you heard it again?

MARY THERESA: Yes. I tried to stay away, but something draws me here. And yes, I've prayed, prayed to drown out the tiny voice, but it does not stop.

MARY COLETTA: Sometimes Satan—

MARY THERESA: No, this is the sweetest most beautiful voice I have ever heard—and yet the saddest.

MARY COLETTA: Do you think it's a message from God?

MARY THERESA: I don't know who it's a message from. Lately, sometimes, even if I don't come out here, I still hear the crying, as if it's echoing throughout the whole convent. I don't know how to stop it from calling out anymore. It follows me everywhere.

MARY COLETTA: You must tell Sister Ursula, immediately.

MARY THERESA: No. *(Pause.)* I know why I hear the cry.

MARY COLETTA: Why?

MARY THERESA: It is my own children—crying out to be born.

MARY COLETTA: That cannot be true.

MARY THERESA: No, it is my children…I could give up everything else—Timothy, family, friends. But I so dearly wanted children. But then, I thought, that would be the ultimate sacrifice, to give up something I wanted so deeply, for the Lord. Now I know, I was wrong. I would be tormented every day I was a nun, and it would not be a willing sacrifice.

MARY COLETTA: There is still time—you may yet pass through this torment. I will pray with you.

MARY THERESA: I have already made up my mind. I cannot stay. Yet, I cannot tell Sister Ursula the real reason. I remember what happened to Mary Felicitus, when she revealed her voices…

MARY COLETTA: And she so wanted to be a nun.

MARY THERESA: So did I…

MARY COLETTA: *(Crying.)* I shall miss you so. *(Takes her hand, then hugs her, crying on her shoulder.)*

MARY THERESA: And I shall miss you too—and this beautiful place.

MARY COLETTA: Once you are gone—I will never know whether you have children or not.

MARY THERESA: I do not know whether I shall be blessed with them either. But I must consider marriage, children, a calling from God also. And that calling is so much louder, so much stronger at this moment, I cannot shut it out any longer.

MARY COLETTA: *(Picks a rose, gives it to Mary Theresa.)* Here— press this in your missalette, and when you pray, remember me.

MARY THERESA: And for you—a leaf from this same rose, to remember me.

MARY COLETTA: A thorn for each of us, to remember our Lord, and His suffering. *(Bell gently rings in distance.)* We better go in, it's almost vesper time.

MARY THERESA: I'm going to stay out here a little longer. Sit by the rock…

(Mary Coletta exits through arbor. Lights slowly dim. Notes from "I Come to the Garden" play, then faintly a far away voice calls almost in time with the bell ringing, "Mama— mama—" Mary Theresa, still sitting on bench, buries head in hands, as lights slowly dim and voice becomes louder.)

Marla's Devotion

Linda Eisenstein

2 Women

Marla (30's) a woman seeking to change her life through spiritual undertakings, and Joey (30's) her lover, a high-energy attorney.

Scene: here & now

> *Marla has been ritualistically prostrating herself over and over again in an effort to gain spiritual insight into life. Her constant need to escape the confines of ennui via such outlandish efforts has threatened to destroy her relationship with the vastly more pragmatic Joey. Here, the two women finally confront their fears and begin the process of reconciliation.*

MARLA: You called my MOTHER?!? Joey, why did you call my MOTHER?!?

JOEY: Baby, I don't have time for...

MARLA: You get home! You get home right now! What the hell are you doing CALLING MY MOTHER!!
(Joey crosses into Marla's space, immediately segueing into their evening argument.)

JOEY: Yeah, I called Arlene. What am I supposed to do ? You've been acting so weird.

MARLA: I'M acting weird! What about you? You're never here. And when you're here you're not here! And when you are here you're angry all the time. All the time!

JOEY: You're goddamn right I'm angry. You wanna know why? Let's hear about Joey's wonderful day at the office. Where a woman had to keep her husband away with a restraining order. And he still beats her within an inch of next Tuesday.

And nobody does shit. Where a dyke losses custody of kid to her lunatic fringe mother-in-law who inhales cigarette smoke and goes to a snake handling church and believes in hitting the kid with a two-by-four because God told her to. And nobody does shit! Who's gonna fight those wars, huh? You oughta be goddamn grateful that somebody is in there punching while you're out here getting all soft and holy and full of *space*. You better pray that everybody like me doesn't get tired of fighting, and gives up to open a bed and break-fast and eat organic oatmeal. Or people like you are gonna be up shit creek without a paddle.

MARLA: But why does it have to hang over us like this? All that anger!

JOEY: It's better than being spaced out!

MARLA: No it isn't! It's choking the breath out of me. It's like I'm breathing in fumes, the whole place is on fire. My God, I have to get close to the ground, just to be able to breathe!

JOEY: Well, pardon me. I just can't put it down, OK? It lives under my skin. And it pays the bills. Which do, by the way, need paying.

MARLA: Oh, you're saying I'm not productive. I'm not a produc-tive member of this household.

JOEY: You said that, Marla, I didn't.

MARLA: My mother wants me to come home, maybe I should.

JOEY: Oh yeah, sure. that really makes sense. That'll certainly make you feel better, living at Arlene's.

MARLA: She offered.

JOEY: Being bundled off to the Methodist sodality, getting intro-duced to eligible guys with pocket protectors, sounds swell. Come on, Marla. What's happening around here?

MARLA: Death is what's happening here! I'm dying!

JOEY: What are you saying? Holy Jesus, Marla, what are you say-ing?!

MARLA: I'm dying. We're dying, Joey. Our relationship is dying and my mother is dying and we're all dying and I'm afraid. I'm afraid all the time. I can't hold on to things, they keep swimming around. I can't freeze them into place. And half the time, I tell you, half the time when I get down, I don't want to get up. I just want to lie there with my face pressed against the floor and cry.

JOEY: Oh, you don't mean dying dying, Jesus, Marla, you scared the living shit out of me. You're talking metaphoric death.

MARLA: No. Literal. It's literal death. With every breath, we're one breath closer to our death, that's a fact, Joey.

JOEY: You're not dying, Marla.

MARLA: Yes we are. We are! Our culture just denies it. The Tibetans know better. When their mothers die, they save the skull and sleep on it for a year for a pillow.

JOEY: Arlene isn't dead, Marla.

MARLA: Imagine that. Sleeping for a year on your mother's skull.

JOEY: She's at the Mall of America, shopping until her feet bleed.

MARLA: You have to wait until it dries out, I guess.

JOEY: Jesus, Marla, is this what you think about all day? You can't go around thinking shit like that! Jesus, I'm calling Dr. Bernstein, you need to go back to her, OK?

MARLA: I won't. This way is better.

JOEY: Bullshit. You need to be on some serious meds, Marla.

MARLA: Everybody we know is on some kind of stupid drug. Does that sound rational? Does that make sense? Everyone gulping anti-depressants, Lithium, Prozac, just to hurl themselves through their ridiculous days? No, thank you.

JOEY: You don't have to feel this way. It's okay to get help, babe.

MARLA: There's something terribly wrong with our culture, Joey.

JOEY: We can't live this way!

MARLA: There goes your face again, Joey. You've got that soap opera look.

JOEY: What? What look?

MARLA: That look. Where you've labeled something and come to a pat conclusion and it makes you feel all better. Because all the ambiguities are set aside. Just like on some stupid soap opera. Like, if our life was a soap opera, right before the commercial break, the music would get all big and soppy.

And I'd say "I'm dying" and the audience would gasp. And they'd find out it was a BRAIN TUMOR and they'd know, ah, *that's* the reason she was acting so weird. It would all be *revealed*. And everyone could breathe easy. They could go, oh, it was a brain tumor, that explains it. Or, oh, she's *depressed*. Like putting a label on it makes anything different or simplifies or explains your life in any way. Or, oh, oh, WE get it, she found out her lover has been sneaking off to a motel with some blond bimbo in pink toenail polish. That's why she was doing all that weird stuff. And they could breathe easy then.

JOEY: Oh, baby…

MARLA: But here? In real life? It's not that simple. You have to decide to breathe easy. When you decide that your life isn't about some external *thing*, some terrible thing that somebody else is or isn't doing, when it's really about how *you* are thinking.

JOEY: Baby, I'm sorry.

MARLA: How you think and breathe in and out each day and construct a world out of your thoughts… Well, that's a different story. That's a whole different plot, see.

JOEY: Marla.

MARLA: It doesn't have a hero or a villain in it. Or a miracle cure. It's not that kind of a story. We're not living in a soap opera, Joey. Are we?

JOEY: No. No, we're not.

MARLA: We're just trying to live…trying to live… *(She begins to cry.)* a life that has some kindness in it.

(Joey goes to her. Holds her through the next.)

JOEY: Sh—sh—sh—. Honey. She doesn't…

(Marla weeps. a long pause as Joey holds her.)

MARLA: This. This is doing me a world of good.

JOEY: I'm sorry.

MARLA: A world of good, Joey.

JOEY: Okay. Sh—sh.

MARLA: It makes me less afraid. It's funny. I said I'm afraid, and I am, but at the same time I've never been less afraid in my life.

JOEY: I love you, Marla.

MARLA: I know. I know. *(The weeping, finally, subsides. A beat.)* You called my mother?

JOEY: Yeah. We actually had a surprisingly nice talk.

MARLA: Huh.

JOEY: We had something to obsess about together. Thinking about you. As the Crawling Lesbian.

MARLA: That's good. That way when I go back to being just an ordinary garden-variety lesbian, with a lawyer lover, she'll actually be relieved.

JOEY: Does this mean you're stopping? Not that I'm asking you to, you understand.

MARLA: No. I'm still getting a lot out of it, actually. You know, you really ought to try it yourself, Joey.

JOEY: Oh, no no no.

MARLA: Really. Once wouldn't kill you, It might just give you...a different perspective.

JOEY: A worm's-eye view.

MARLA: A caterpillar's anyway.

JOEY: One caterpillar at a time is enough around here.

MARLA: Caterpillars turn into butterflies.

JOEY: They fly away, is that what you mean? Flap their wings and take off for parts unknown.

MARLA: Are we talking about you, or me?

JOEY: Marla, I'm not going anywhere. I don't know about you, though. You're changing.

MARLA: Yes. Yes, I am.

JOEY: And when you turn into something too different—I think you're going to want a different view.

MARLA: I do. I have longed for a different view. That's why I'm down here. *(Beat.)* You might like it. It really doesn't hurt that much. *(Beat.)* Especially with kneepads. *(Beat.)*

JOEY: A couple of times, okay? But I don't have to be a believer, you're not gonna make me one, okay?

MARLA: I don't want to make you anything. Just try it out a couple of times. *(Pause.)* How could it hurt?

(Joey tries it once.)

JOEY: Jesus. This is like pushups. I feel like I'm in the Army or something.

MARLA: No hurry. We're not trying to build up our muscles, really. Just our intentions. That's hard enough.

JOEY: Okay, so—

MARLA: Look around. It's kinda cool isn't it?

JOEY: I really don't like all the looking down. I'd rather look up, I think.

MARLA: So stop for a minute and roll over.

(Joey rolls on her back.)

JOEY: God, that's better. What's that on the ceiling? Cobwebs?

MARLA: I haven't really been looking up there lately. My attention has been elsewhere.

JOEY: No shit. *(Pause.)* Mine, too.

(Joey and Marla lie on their backs, looking at the ceiling. Their heads are close together.)

JOEY: I don't really feel like getting up.

MARLA: Me neither.

JOEY: I should, you know, I gotta...

(Marla leans up on one elbow.)

MARLA: Shh. Take your time.

(Joey looks at Marla a long time. She strokes Marla's hair. Marla smiles. Lights start to fade.)

MARLA: Take your time.

The Ornamental Hermit

Jocelyn Beard

2 Women
Lily Mountfleurry (18) the frustrated daughter of a planter and
Mehitable (18) her personal maid and best friend.

Scene: Rivermede Plantation, South Carolina, 1856

> *When Lily returns from her trip to Charleston, she discovers
> that her father has written from England that her Temple of
> Aphrodite—a structure that she designed and had con-
> structed in the garden—is to be destroyed. Tempestuous Lily
> has vowed to live in the ruins of her temple with her house
> slave, Mehitable, until her father returns home from a trip
> abroad and can explain himself. Her, Lily and Mehitable pass
> a dark night together in the ruins, revealing that there is
> more to their relationship than that of mistress and slave.*

> *Lily and Mehitable huddle under blankets as Lily reads aloud
> by lantern light. Joe sits quietly, unseen by either of the
> women, in the shadows.*

LILY: *(Reading.)* "No!" cried the fair Melvina as Siegfried collapsed
to the floor, his hands clutching in vain at the knife that had
been thrust into his beating heart..."
(Mehitable shrieks and clutches at her own chest.)
LILY: "No !" cried she again as the villain fled the turret."
MEHITABLE: He dead, Miss Lily?
LILY: *(Turning a page.)* Don't be so goulish, Mehitable! And please
say, "Is he dead." Not "He dead."
MEHITABLE: Well, is he? Dead?
LILY: Of course not. *(Returning to the book.)* "Siegfried!" she

gasped as she sank to the cold stone floor by his side, the blood draining from her pretty face. "Siegfried, my love! What manner of man has committed so foul a deed on this dark and dismal night? Oh, my dearest heart, Siegfried, will you not speak?"

(There is a low rumble of thunder in the distance.)

MEHITABLE: *(Looking around fearfully.)* Storm's comin'.

LILY: Let it. *(Reading.)* "His eyes quivered and opened, and Melvina saw within their tortured depths the very lodestone of human despair." Oh, Mehitable, is that not the most profound turn of phrase you have ever in your life heard? "The very lodestone of human despair." Is that not eloquent to bursting?

MEHITABLE: What's it mean, Miss Lily?

LILY: It means...well, Mehitable, a lodestone is a...well, it's really more of a ...oh, never mind!

(More distant thunder.)

MEHITABLE: It's gonna rain on our heads, Miss Lily.

LILY: Oh, so what if it does, Mehitable? Rain is just water and I am led to believe that we are quite filled with water so it can't possibly hurt us. Now, if you don't mind... *(She returns to reading the book.)* "Siegfried!" she gasped. "You live! Oh, my Siegfried!"

MEHITABLE: Beggin' you pardon, Mistress Lily, but why does she keep callin' him that name?

LILY: What name?

MEHITABLE: Zig-freed.

LILY: Oh, for heaven's sake. It's his name. Just like my name is Lily and yours is Mehitable.

MEHITABLE: But, my mammy named me...

LILY: I know very well what that foolish woman named you, Mehitable, and I must inform you yet again that *(Pronounced with great distaste.)* "Delilah" is an altogether inappropriate name for a young woman in your position. The Biblical Delilah was an evil temptress! Why your mammy decided to name you after such a low-born woman I'll never know. Now...

MEHITABLE: Then what about Siegfried? Who did his mammy name him after?

LILY: Mehitable, "Siegfried" is just a name. *(Lily rises and acts out all of the following, including Mehitable in her various pantomimes.)* It's passionate: "The *coup de gras* was delivered by the noble Count Siegfried," *(Lily pantomimes running Mehitable through.)* "Thunderstruck, Siegfried swept the lovely young peasant woman into his manly arms." *(Lily grabs a giggling Mehitable and sweeps her into a dip.)* It is refined: "Siegfried savored the fine claret as he considered the couples swirling around the dance floor." *(Mehitable pantomimes swaggering and sipping from a claret glass while Lily swirls around in a waltz.)* And above all, Mehitable, it's mysterious: Where is this man named Siegfried from? Who can say? Perhaps a remote castle high in the Prussian Alps where he broods over a lost love under stormy cold skies. *(Lily puts her arm around Mehitable and both young women gaze up into the night sky.)* Can't you see him up there on the battlements, Mehitable? Brooding away? Or better yet in the court of a mad king, where he alone defends the crown from traitors and assassins! *En garde*, dog, and prepare to breathe your last! *(Mehitable shrieks as Lily pursues her with an invisible sword. They collapse, laughing, in the bed clothes.)* Oh, Mehitable, Siegfried is simply the most romantic name in the world.

MEHITABLE: *(Panting and thoroughly unconvinced.)* Then how come there ain't no Siegfrieds 'round here?

LILY: You are impossible, Mehitable! *(With a casual glance in Joe's direction.)* I suppose you think "Joe" is the most romantic of all names.

MEHITABLE: *(Embarrassed.)* No, I do not!

LILY: Oh, I'm sure the feeling is mutual. I am certain that Joe thinks Mehitable is the most romantic name in the world... *(Calling over her shoulder.)* Don't you, Joe?

178 women's scenes

MEHITABLE: Miss Lily! Please…

LILY: Oh, all right, all right, Mehitable… *(Lowering her voice.)* But you don't think he's been out here all night every night keeping watch over me, do you?

(Mehitable glances over her shoulder at Joe's dark form.)

MEHITABLE: *(Loudly.)* I swear I don't know what that stupid man thinks he's doin'. He can die from a night chill for all I think 'bout it.

LILY: Mehitable!

MEHITABLE: It's God's truth, Miss Lily! *(Making it up as she goes along.)* That old Joe is sittin' out there like a big dumb owl cause I find out that he's been keepin' time with little Gabby when me with you in Charlestontown!

LILY: What! Gabby the seamstress with the squinty eye?

MEHITABLE: He can just sit out here 'til the Lord above calls Judgment Day for all I think about it and that is the truth you can put in the ground!

LILY: My! Well, let's ignore the rogue, then, shall we?

MEHITABLE: We shall.

(Both women turn back to the book in a huff. More distant thunder.)

LILY: Back to Siegfried…where were we…here it is: "Tears slid like pearls down her fair, colorless cheeks as she clasped his bloodied hand to her heart. "Yes, my dearest Siegfried. I have escaped the unspeakable subterranean chamber of the dread Lord Montfort aided by your brother…your own dear Helmut…who gave his life this very night so that I could now hold you in my arms here in the safety of…

BOTH: *(Laughing.)* Bubenschloss!"

LILY: "The brave hero gazed into his true love's deep sapphire eyes, which brimmed with diamonds of tears…" Diamonds of tears. Is that not beautiful, Mehitable? *(Back to book.)* "…which brimmed with diamonds of tears, and he was made to think of his dear, brave brother, Helmut…so tall, so noble. Dead." Is that romantic?

MEHITABLE: Not if he's dead, Miss Lily.

LILY: (Reading.) "No man shall ever love as I have loved," whispered Siegfried..."

MEHITABLE: Uh-oh.

LILY: Uh-oh? What do you mean, uh-oh?

MEHITABLE: Poor Mister Siegfried's a gonner, Mistress, just like his brother: tall, noble dead Helmut.

LILY: Don't be ridiculous, Mehitable. The hero never, ever dies.

MEHITABLE: Well, this one's gonna.

LILY: He never will! Cousin Bettina sent me this book all the way from London, England, Mehitable, and she informed me in her kind letter that this particular volume is universally admired by all young ladies in London society and is generally considered to be the most romantic story ever set down on paper. Do you imagine, Mehitable, that the most romantic story ever set down on paper would include the most unfortunate detail of a deceased hero? You are simply goulish to the point of distraction! (Returning to the book.) Now, where the hell was I? Ah, yes. (She takes a moment to recapture the romantic mood.) "No man shall ever love as I have loved," whispered Siegfried. "Helmut! I follow thee!" The brave Siegfried then gave a cry and gave himself over to greedy death while still in her trembling arms" WHAT???
(There is another rumble of thunder and the pale flash of distant lightning.)

MEHITABLE: (Laughing.) I told you! I told you he were a gonner! Poor Mister Siegfried. Both him and his brother be dead and fair Melvina's left all alone to cry her diamond tears.

LILY: Well this is simply the most horrible, nasty, vile book it has ever been my misfortune to read! I am going to write to Cousin Bettina first thing in the morning and tell her so! Ugh!
(She tosses the offending tome into the darkness. More distant thunder.)

MEHITABLE: Mistress Lily?

LILY: Yes, Mehitable?

MEHITABLE: I was wondren, Mistress, if you woulda really done what you said th'other day?

LILY: Done what?

MEHITABLE: Would you a switched me? Like you said you would?

LILY: Dear Lord spare me! Of course not! What a terrible thought for you to be carrying around in your heart against me!

MEHITABLE: But you said…

LILY: I know what I said, Mehitable! What you have got to understand is exactly how…how provoked I was when I saw what had been done to my lovely temple of Aphrodite.

(More thunder and lightning. The storm is getting a bit closer.)

MEHITABLE: So you didn't mean that thing you said…'bout switchin' me?

LILY: Of course not. Have I once in all my life, to your knowledge, ever switched anyone or anything besides that lazy old chestnut gelding's behind?

MEHITABLE: No…

LILY: I abhor violence. Simply abhor it! I hate the way…well, the way things are…here, well not exactly here, at Rivermede… we treat you well do we not?

MEHITABLE: Yes, mistress.

LILY: *(Lowering her voice.)* Why over at Green Hill I hear there are regular beatings now. That awful Mr. Frack once whipped a man to death! Right in front of everyone! Including the ladies!

MEHITABLE: *(Quietly.)* I heard that, too.

LILY: but we don't conduct ourselves in such a barbaric manner here at Rivermede, do we?

MEHITABLE: No, mistress.

LILY: Indeed we do not! And we never will. It isn't in our nature. That absurd Mr. Seely has suggested to me on more than one occasion that I am ignorant in such matters but I am not! I am well aware of the international debate over the keeping of slaves. I know what's being said. I hear the rattling sabers just as keenly as anyone. I know these things because I listen, Mehitable. I listen to the foolish little boys who fancy themselves young men when they gather for their cigars and their brandy. They talk and they talk about the "evil" north and its anti-slave militias and its grim little spinsters who host tea parties in Boston at which abolition is discussed like…like the weather. I know all about the abolitionist war in Kansas Territory. I have heard about the runaways who make it all the way to Canada…and I have heard about the ones who don't. Why, I'll have you know that my Cousin Odette belongs to several anti-slavery groups in Richmond and I say, good for her! *(Lowering her voice.)* Good for her. Mr. Seely is wrong, Mehitable, I do know about these things. But all the knowing doesn't do any good, does it? One deprived of power can put knowledge to little good use. *(More thunder and a flash of lightning.)* Sometimes, Mehitable, I feel the tides of an anger so vast and so consuming that it's pulling everything apart. It's a terrifying thing to think about, and the terror is made more sweet by the fact that thinking about it is all I am permitted to do! Lord help me! *(Focusing on Mehitable.)* That, however, is all besides the point Mehitable, which is that I would never, ever lay a hand on you or on anyone. Especially not you. You're my…if it wasn't for you… well, it's just that I was so angry about my temple.

MEHITABLE: Your lettin' yourself get too distressed about these rocks.

LILY: That temple was the only thing in this world that was mine, Mehitable, totally mine. Who am I in this house? The useless, worthless daughter, that's who. I may as well be a house girl like you!

MEHITABLE: Now you stop that, Miss Lily!

LILY: I am an expense—just as you are. Something to be balanced against a ledger. Nothing here is mine. Nothing. but the temple. I conceived of it! I drew the plans. I directed the men…it was my *accomplishment*. It was something that was supposed to say something about me forever. Dear Lord above, I loved that temple!

MEHITABLE: Stop it now. You know as well as me that you can't be lovin' a pile of rocks.

LILY: *(With a sigh.)* Why not?

MEHITABLE: Ain't you never once been in love with a man, Miss Lily?

LILY: *(After a moment.)* Once. Once I was.
(More thunder.)

MEHITABLE: Who with? Ain't not a single man 'round here you spend more'n a minute in his company, beyond Mr. Seely.

LILY: Oh, that ridiculous man!

MEHITABLE: *(Excitedly.)* Who then? I can't believe that you have such a secret, Miss Lily!

LILY: Oh, all right, Mehitable! *(Settling into a special memory.)* When I was a young girl—thirteen, I was that summer—I traveled abroad with Daddy and Mother to visit Cousin Melville Montfleurry at Drummond Hall in Yorkshire. Lovely, lovely Yorkshire.

MEHITABLE: Yorkshire a nice place?

LILY: Yorkshire is…well it's another world from here, Mehitable. It's like a dream. And Drummond Hall is like the heart of a dream.

MEHITABLE: Tell me about the man, Miss Lily.

LILY: Well, one day I was out exploring the gardens. Drummond Hall is an entire universe of lovely gardens. And no slaves, Mehitable!

MEHITABLE: No slaves?

LILY: Not a one.

MEHITABLE: They got black folk in Yorkshire?

LILY: Well, no. No black folk. The British don't keep slaves as we do.

MEHITABLE: Why not?

LILY: In any case, Mehitable, it was a lovely summer day in Yorkshire. Everything was green and cool and sweet-scented. I found myself sittin' beneath an old willow tree next to a brook just thinking how lovely the world can be, when suddenly I heard a terrible commotion.

MEHITABLE: What was it?

LILY: A group of boys—savage little brutes—were chasing a tiny dog, about this big. (She extends her hands to indicate a toy sized dog.)

MEHITABLE: Oh, Miss Lily! You know I love little dogs! What did you do??

LILY: Well, the leader of the boys, a most unpleasant red-haired youth covered in freckles, caught the dog. "Cut off its head!" one of them yelled. "Cut off its tail!"

MEHITABLE: No!

LILY: Yes! I scrambled to my feet. I was going to stop those boys… no matter what. I took a step forward, when suddenly I felt a strong hand grasp my arm. A deep voice said, "You stay here, lady."

MEHITABLE: Ooooh, Miss Lily!!

LILY: And then he was past me, moving across the brook. That terrible older boy with the freckles looked up and the look on his cruel little pinched face…it was as if he beheld the devil himself in all his finery!

MEHITABLE: Oh, save us, Miss Lily!

LILY: And then I heard that voice again, that wonderfully deep voice. "Go home, Thomas Banks. Go home, all of you. If I catch you on Drummond land again, poaching pooches, I'll have your hides for cloth." That wretched boy dropped the dog and they just ran.

MEHITABLE: This man saved the little dog?

LILY: He did, Mehitable. As if that dog was worth all the tea in China. He picked that scared little beast up in his arms and then turned to me, smiled and just before he crossed the brook, asked "Are ye fairy or are ye angel?" "Neither of those, Sir," I replied. "Nay," he said, "I'm thinking ye be both." And off he walked, into the dappled sunlight of that summer day.

MEHITABLE: Who was he?

LILY: Benjamin Strong. A tenant on the estate. A good man. Not at all like the lazy bantycocks who strut themselves around the Carolinas. A man of feeling and substance.

MEHITABLE: *(Sagely.)* So, you're in love with Benjamin Strong.

LILY: Benjamin Strong. I never even saw his face. But yes, I suppose I am in love with him or someone like him. Someone I probably will never meet.

(More thunder and lightning.)

MEHITABLE: *(After a moment.)* I am sorry 'bout your temple. Miss Lily. It was like…the heart of a dream. *(A ray of hope.)* Mister Seely is just chompin' at the bit to build you a new one. I hate sleepin' out here in this hainty old place.

(More thunder and lightning. Closer still.)

LILY: I keep telling you it isn't haunted, isn't that right, Joe? And we have to stay here. It's a matter of pride, Mehitable.

MEHITABLE: Just look where all that pride got Mister Siegfried.

(Lily chuckles despite herself.)

MEHITABLE: *(Looking off.)* Uh-oh…here come Missus!

LILY: *(As she blows out the lantern.)* Quick, Mehitable! Pretend we're sleeping and she'll go away!

(Lily and Mehitable hunker down into their blankets. More thunder and lightning.)

TropicAna

Diana Montané

2 Women
Ana Mendieta (36) Cuban-American sculptor, a woman possessed by her passion for art, and Liz/Raquel (30's)

Scene: NYC

> *Liz is the Assistant D.A. assigned to investigate the suspicious death of Ana Mendieta. Her investigation into the life of the tempestuous artist has introduced her to a side of NYC art world that she never dreamed existed. Here, Liz muses about Ana and her thoughts drift to the time when Ana first arrived in America with her sister, Raquel, whom Liz becomes in the fantasy.*

ANA: *(Rising from the tableaux.)* Pssst! I'm alive! And I am TropicAna! *(Liz walks over to her. Sinead O'Connor's "Just Like You Said It Would" plays.)*

ANA: Will you be my mama? Will you be my sister? Will you be Raquel? Rocky? Raquelín-pin-pin?

LIZ: The first DA was in charge of the Domestic Violence Unit. I've always wondered about the circumstances that prepare the ground for domestic violence, and how much the degrees of violence are inextricably tied to those circumstances. What do you want from me, Ana?

ANA: Pain of Cuba, orphanhood I am. I'm *Anita la Huerfanita*. I'm little Orphan Annie. Will you be my *mami*?

LIZ: I am trying to defend you! We're not going to gain anything from these postponement tactics.

ANA: there are rats in this place!

LIZ: You're dead now and I don't believe in you. Go away.

ANA: Come with me to the window. See how high the window-sill is? I can do it if I have a ledge!

LIZ: You don't have a ledge, Ana. You don't have a leg to stand on. I want to defend you! I do believe in you and we need to win this! It could have been any of us! It could happen to someone else! Goddamnit, I'm going to lose this case, aren't I!

ANA: *(A child's tantrum.)* No, no, no, no, no! I want to get out of here! Why did *mami* and *papi* send us here alone?

LIZ: *(Transforming slowly into Raquel.)* They wanted to save you, Ani, just like I did. They wanted to give you a chance to live.

ANA: Why, why, why, why, why?

RAQUEL: To get us out of Cuba. To give us wings to fly.

ANA: Wait! I hid some of my drawings! Do you have earth from Cuba and sand from Varadero?

RAQUEL: I have the two bags we brought on the plane.

ANA: Get them while I get my pad! We're going to make a beach!

RAQUEL: Every summer we went to our grandmother's house on the beach. We spent all day in the sand and in the water. Ana would make these fantastic sand silhouettes of women with big breast and buttocks.

(Ana comes in with the pad.)

RAQUEL: And you floated in the water and you wanted me to cover you with seashells and flowers. Do you remember?

ANA: And you played the piano and I could hear you all the way down at the beach till it got drowned by the sound of the waves. I want to go home, Rocky.

RAQUEL: I do too, Ani. I want to play *Moonlight Sonata*.

ANA: *(Begins to draw furiously.)* I want my images to have power! To be magic!

RAQUEL: Let me see. This looks like Yemayá, the Goddess of the Waters. *(Yemayá appears slowly and watches silently over them.)* Can I have it?

ANA: No, no, no, no, no. One day I'm going to be famous and my paintings will sell for thousands and thousands of dollars. Then I'll give you one. So you can have lots and lots of kids and a big back yard and two dogs. and then I'll come and visit you and everybody will look at you and say, "That is Ana Mendieta's sister." And you'll have a piano and give a big concert and I'll come see you and we'll be on TV. The nuns won't let me watch TV because I was screaming in our room!

RAQUEL: Ani, you can't scream every time we get a letter from home.

ANA: But I want to see *mami* and *abuela* and *abuelo* and our cousins and I want to go home. It's so cold here! Where are the bags?

RAQUEL: Oh, I think Sister Louise confiscated them.

ANA: She banged my head against the door knob. See? It made my nose bleed.

RAQUEL: Well, we can pretend. They can't take pretend away. Lie down. *(Yemayá begins a slow and innocent dance of waves.)* You are floating in the water. It is the bluest water anybody ever saw, of the first blue that was ever created. And you can see the bottom, and the ivory sand covered with the most beautiful iridescent shells in the world. *(Ana is lying down and Raquel pretends to cover her with seashells and flower petals.)*

RAQUEL: *(To the audience.)* When we were at St. Mary's orphanage, Ana was very rebellious. But she had a natural wit and she was devilish, like a little imp. And she could invent people, she really could. She called Sister Louise "The Penguin" from the Batman comic-books. She could make a myth out of almost anything.

(Ana rises suddenly and gives Raquel a start. Yemayá stops dancing, also startled.)

RAQUEL: Ay, Ani, you scared me!

(Yemayá remains on stage, taking a silent part in the scene, often laughing.)

ANA: *(Uncovering her shoulder.)* You see this mark? That's because God was going to make me black and then he changed his mind! Now I'm waiting for Him to finish the job!

RAQUEL: Girl, you ain't black! You Cuban! You Spanish! You come from Spain!

ANA: I come from Africa! Spanish people are bad! They brought the slaves to Cuba and killed the Indians and the gypsies. Now we kill them! Queen Isabella is a ho!

RAQUEL: You a ho!

(Voices in the background begin chanting like a chorus.)

VOICES: Nigger...whore...spic...nigger...whore...spic...nigger...whore...spic...

ANA: I be a nigger and a spic and a ho!

(Voices continue with the beat of Afro-Cuban drums. Yemayá moves spasmodically.)

ANA: I know! I'm going to go back and seduce Fidel Castro and then kill him! Then we can go home! Let's rehearse!

RAQUEL: I don't know how to, Ani.

ANA: Pretend! *(She affects an official voice.)* The *señorita* Mendieta is here to see the Commander-in-Chief.

RAQUEL: *(Trying to imitate Castro.)* Niña...what do you want with me?

ANA: You're a hero of the people.

RAQUEL: But you left.

ANA: They made me, Fidel. My parents sent me and my sister away alone without our consent. They said we'd be like Peter Pan. I want to be here with you. Can I come home?

RAQUEL: Nah. You're with the *americanos* now. You better stay there.

ANA: Shit, I'm tired of this game! I want to go to Varadero! *(She lies down again.)*

RAQUEL: The next four and a half years, until our mother's arrival in this country, became a nightmare of fear, alienation, racism, accusations, loneliness, misunderstanding, and a loss of human respect and freedom as we were shuffled through orphanages, boarding schools and foster homes. Eight in all.

ANA: Rocky, I can't fall asleep.

RAQUEL: Try, Ani.

ANA: *(In a scary voice.)* Do you know the rats blow on you before they bite so that you don't feel their teeth in the night?

RAQUEL: Ay ya, coño! Go to sleep!

ANA: What is this Dubuque, Iowa? This building is made of stone! It is crushing me! The nuns are mean! They can't crush me! We have to get away!

RAQUEL: Where to, Ana?

ANA: *(Laughing.)* To Havana, fucking banana! *(Yemayá flees, laughing obscenely. Quick blackout.)*

MEN'S SCENES

Dave's Pocket

David Stirling

2 men

Dave 1 (30's) and Dave 2 (30's) Best friends facing an insur-
mountable crisis.

Scene: the United Kingdom

> Dave and Dave have been comedy partners and best friends
> for many years. When Dave 1's wife leaves him, he turns to
> Dave 2 for comfort and finds much more than he bargained
> for: the truth.

> Straight into SX. Door chime, followed by loud knocking. The
> lights are off. Dave 2 appears. He has clearly got dressed in a
> hurry. He freezes. More knocking. Dave 2 switches on the
> light and answers the door. Dave 1 enters.

DAVE 1: It's Judy. She's walked out again.

DAVE 2: I know…She called me.

DAVE 1: Do you know where she is?

DAVE 2: Have you tried her mother's?

DAVE 1: The bitch wouldn't speak to me.

DAVE 2: With an attitude like that, it's hardly surprising.

DAVE 1: You don't have Edith for a mother-in-law.

DAVE 2: She seemed nice at the wedding.

DAVE 1: Everyone's nice at your wedding. It's part of the trap.

DAVE 2: Look, Dave, this is a little awkward for me…

DAVE 1: I know. You're Judy's friend as well…

DAVE 2: That as well of course, and I know you probably need a
friend right now, but, what I mean is this is not a very good
time for me.

(SX. Shower being switched on in another room.)

DAVE 2: I've got company…

DAVE 1: Oh, I see. God, sorry. I should have rung first.

DAVE 2: That's OK. But maybe you should go home. She might be trying to call.

DAVE 1: I could really do with a drink. Just one and then I'll go. I promise.

DAVE 2: Alright, just one.

(Dave two pours one drink.)

DAVE 1: Hard at it, were you? You and Annie?

DAVE 2: Not exactly…Annie's at a conference in Wales.

DAVE 1: You sly old dog, you. So who is it? Is it the one from make-up with the big…

DAVE 2: No, it's not her.

DAVE 1: So who is it?

DAVE 2: Just drop it, Dave.

DAVE 1: It's not bloke is it?

DAVE 2: No, it's not a bloke.

DAVE 1: Sorry, but me and Judy did always wonder…I mean, why you and Annie never took the plunge…

DAVE 2: Well, you and Judy can stop wondering. You're entitled to Scotch and sympathy, but my love life is none of your business.

DAVE 1: Why won't you tell me? Do I know her?

DAVE 2: She's married, OK?

DAVE 1: Christ, that's a bit low, isn't it? Hopping on someone's wife the moment Annie's out the door.

DAVE 2: When it comes to extra-curricular leg-overs, you're hardly one to preach, are you? Come off it, Dave. The tit-lady in make-up's about the only one that you haven't made. You're famous for it. It's a studio joke…Dave nipping back to make-up for a bit more 'puffy, luv', spelt with a hyphen.

DAVE 1: I never used a hyphen.

DAVE 2: Can't you take anything seriously? For God's sake…

DAVE 1: Your high moral tone's a touch ironic under the circumstances, wouldn't you say?

194 men's scenes

DAVE 2: Some of your conquests were barely out of knee-socks.

DAVE 1: I happen to like knee-socks.

DAVE 2: You're incredible, you know that?

DAVE 1: So they tell me.

DAVE 2: You're just a fucking whore.

Dave 1: Is there any other kind?

DAVE 2: Don't you care about anyone?

DAVE 1: I care enough to be careful and not get found out. No one's ever walked in on me with my trousers down.

DAVE 2: Yeah, but everybody knows, Dave. You're a walking hard-on. You go around grinning like a panda that just had a blow-job. People talk in this business, Dave. And, believe me, they talk about you all the time.

DAVE 1: Judy doesn't know.

DAVE 2: David, she's left you.

DAVE 1: Judy doesn't know. Things have just been difficult since the twins were born, she'll be back. It's a post-natal thing.

DAVE 2: Your arrogance is staggering, you know that? The twins were born over a year ago.

DAVE 1: I'm telling you, she doesn't know.

DAVE 2: David, believe me. She knows.

DAVE 1: And how do you come to be the fountain of knowledge on the subject?

DAVE 2: She told me.

DAVE 1: You know where she is, don't you?

(Dave 2 makes no reply.)

DAVE 1: Just who the hell have you got upstairs?

DAVE 2: I don't think she wants to see you.

DAVE 1: I don't care what you think. She's my bloody wife and I'll speak to her where and when I fucking please.

DAVE 2: You stupid bastard! Maybe that's why she left you. She's put up with you for years— Christ, one way or another you've screwed just about everyone. But she put up with it. Maybe in the end she just got tired of being "your bloody wife."

DAVE 1: You jumped-up little bastard.

(Dave 1 moves to hit Dave 2, then stops.)

DAVE 2: Get out of my flat.

DAVE 1: That's my wife you've got upstairs.

DAVE 2: Maybe you should ask her about that.

DAVE 1: I already did. Eight years ago. She said "I do."

DAVE 2: Well, she's changed her mind. She's staying here, Dave.

DAVE 1: With you? Don't make me laugh.

DAVE 2: I'm tired of making you laugh. You know that? I've had enough of writing gags for some overblown stooge. I'm tired of you lording your fame about, fucking every gullible little fool you come across like you had something to do with it. But you, you're just a fucking mouthpiece, and don't you forget it.

DAVE 1: Just listen to yourself.

DAVE 2: I am. It's the first honest thing I've said in years.

DAVE 1: Have you just slept with my wife? *(Dave 2 makes no reply.)* You little hypocrite. Exactly how long have you been screwing my wife?

DAVE 2: Just over half an hour, and it was great. You know what Judy told me? She said it was nice to have sex with someone who was in the same room for a change.

DAVE 1: Well, enjoy it while it lasts, 'cos it doesn't last long. She doesn't love you, you know. She just feels sorry for you. She always did. That's probably why she slept with you.

DAVE 2: Get out of my flat. Just get the fuck out, and get the fuck out of my life.

DAVE 1: Christ, that's ironic. We've been trying to get rid of you for years but you keep coming back for more, you kept clinging on. You're the parasite, that's what you are. You hung around our house like a bad smell.

DAVE 2: And who paid for your house? It was me, me and my scripts. You're the parasite. Everything you ever said, I wrote.

DAVE 1: You only wrote down what I said in the first place, so enough of this great writer crap. You're a crappy little writer who writes crappy little sitcoms.

DAVE 2: Let's see how far you get without my crappy little sit-coms.

DAVE 1: I'll get on just fine. You'll see, without me you're nothing.

DAVE 2: No, without Judy, I'm nothing. I love her, Dave. I think I always loved her.

DAVE 1: So did I...once.

DAVE 2: I know you did, I know. I'm sorry.
(Pause.)

DAVE 2: I think you'd better go now.

DAVE 1: Do you know where she left the kids?

DAVE 2: They're at Edith's. I don't think she'll let you in, though, because—

DAVE 1: She's a bitch.

DAVE 2: Yeah, something like that.

DAVE 1: Christ, Dave, why did it have to be you.
(Exits.)

The Legacy

Mark Harelik

2 men
Dave (40's) a man whose wife is dying and Nathan (12) his son.

Scene: a small town in West Texas, 1962

As Jews living on the Texas prairie, Dave's family has faced many obstacles. Now Dave must tell Nathan that his mother is dying of cancer.

O O O

Nathan is sitting on the stairs. Dave carefully steps by him and carries Rachel off to the bedroom. Nathan doesn't move.

DAVE: Sell my crawdads three for a dime, honey
Sell my crawdads three for a dime, oh babe
Sell my crawdads three for a dime
Your crawdad ain't as good as mine
Honey, baby mine
(Nathan sits in silence for a bit, then Dave returns.)
DAVE: Bar mitzvah stuff sounds good.
NATHAN: I need to pee.
DAVE: I'll wait here if you want to come back.
NATHAN: I want to pee in the bushes.
DAVE: Good idea. Let's pee in the bushes.
(They go out to the bushes that ring the porch.)
NATHAN: Why did Mom scream?
DAVE: She's scared.
NATHAN: Scared of what?
(Pause.)
DAVE: Do you do this a lot?
NATHAN: If I really have to go? From the roof, yeah.

DAVE: I wondered what was wrong with the grass. When you have your bar mitzvah,...

NATHAN: Yeah?

DAVE: They say, "Today you are a man."

NATHAN: Yeah, but they don't really mean it.

DAVE: I grew up in this house, too, you know. I peed off the roof.

NATHAN: No, you didn't . Did you?

DAVE: Are you kiddin' me? When I was twelve, I was the spittin' image of you.

NATHAN: Peanut?

DAVE: Just exactly like you, my man. Aunt Sarah's going to be staying on here for a bit.

NATHAN: Whose great idea was that?

DAVE: Mom is sick.

NATHAN: I know.

DAVE: She's not gonna get better.

NATHAN: Yes, she is.

DAVE: Maybe six months, maybe a year, she's gonna die.
(Pause.)

NATHAN: No, she's not.

DAVE: It's a terrible thing, bud, but she needs us to be strong.

NATHAN: She's just sick for a little bit.

DAVE: No. The doctors all say so and the doctors are right. It's lousy for a little kid to have to go through this, but it's even lousier for Mom. And we gotta help her. So you need to be a man. Now. And for the next little while. Schoolwork. No complaints. Quiet around the house. Bar mitzvah. Every day, there'll be a time afterwards when you can go back to being a little kid, but right now we need you to be a man.
(Lightning. Dave looks up.)

NATHAN: How can you say that about Mom?

DAVE: Because it's the truth, sweetie.

NATHAN: You're full of poop! She's not gonna die!

DAVE: I hate it, too.

NATHAN: You're full of poop!

DAVE: We have to stick together, Nate.

NATHAN: You didn't pee off the roof! You didn't do anything!

DAVE: Come here, sweetie.

NATHAN: What's she sick from?

DAVE: Cancer.

NATHAN: Then why don't you look sad?

DAVE: I'm very sad.

NATHAN: She's not gonna die, Dad!

DAVE: We have to face reality, Nate.

(Nathan rushes inside. Dave remains in the yard.)

NATHAN: You don't know what's real!

DAVE: Yes, I do, sweetie. I do know!

(Dave looks up at the sky. He opens his mouth, as though to call out, then with great effort, composes himself again. There is a low rumble of thunder.)

Molly's Delicious

Craig Wright

2 Men

Allan "Lindy" Linda (50's) a man greeting his niece's young suitor, and Alec (18) the suitor in question: a young mortician in love.

Scene: an apple orchard in Pine City, MN, 1965

> *When Alec comes a'courting Lindy's pregnant niece, the apple grower does his best to determine the serious young man's intentions.*

○ ○ ○

ALEC: Good afternoon Mr. Linda.

LINDY: Good afternoon, Mr. Burnside. You can call me "Lindy."

ALEC: Sir, I know this'll seem old fashioned, but I've never been that comfortable calling my elders by their given names.

LINDY: And I've never been that comfortable with anyone calling me "Mr. Linda." It's an unfortunate Finnish name, Alec. I wear it with shame. There's no point in dwelling on it.

ALEC: If you hate it so much, why don't you change it?

LINDY: For all intents and purposes, Alec, I have. Call me "Lindy."

ALEC: Yes sir.

LINDY: Lindy.

ALEC: Lindy.

LINDY: You want an apple?

ALEC: No, thank you, sir, I just brushed my teeth.

LINDY: Then I'll set you up with a bushel when you go.

ALEC: We've still got a whole bushel at home, sir.

LINDY: What's the matter, you don't like apples?

ALEC: No sir, I like them. I'd take another bushel.

LINDY: Good.

(Brief pause.)

LINDY: Those wouldn't happen to be funeral flowers, would they?

ALEC: No. That'd be kind of creepy anyway, wouldn't it?

LINDY: That's exactly what I was gonna say.

(Brief pause.)

LINDY: What did you think of Paster Ed's sermon this morning?

ALEC: I don't know.

LINDY: He's lobbying pretty hard for that shopping mall, don't you think?

ALEC: I guess so.

LINDY: If I were him, I'd be ashamed, I mean, three Sundays in a row now he's twisted the gospel into an argument on behalf of that monstrosity.

ALEC: They're saying there'd be a Chinese restaurant.

LINDY: Yeah, well, I don't like Chinese food much, do you?

ALEC: I like it ok.

LINDY: And I suppose you think church is a place for playing politics too?

ALEC: No—

LINDY: And streetlights all over town, that was his idea too, wasn't it, you like the streetlights?

ALEC: No!

LINDY: He shouldn't've brought out that blueprint, Alec! The altar's no place for a blueprint!

ALEC: I—I agree.

(Brief pause.)

LINDY: You got a draft card?

ALEC: Yes sir.

LINDY: That's good.

ALEC: Is Alison here?

LINDY: Why do you want to know?

(For an instant, we hear Cindy and Alison yelling at each other in the house.)

[CINDY: *(Offstage.)* Young lady, you will not wear that Coast Guard sweatshirt!]

[ALISON: *(Offstage.)* I'll wear whatever I want, you old weirdo!]

202 men's scenes

[CINDY: *(Offstage.)* You will not and don't you dare talk to me that way!]

[ALISON: *(Offstage.)* I wish I was dead!]

[CINDY: *(Offstage.)* I wish you were too, at least then I could get you dressed!]

(Sound of breaking glass. Lindy slides the cap on and begins slowly screwing down the press.)

LINDY: Girl talk. Look, Alec, do you really have any—feelings towards Alison?

ALEC: What do you mean, sir?

LINDY: I mean I assume you've got intentions, coming here, Alec, but do you actually have any feelings for Alison?

ALEC: I don't really know her that well, yet, sir, to say.

LINDY: No, you don't, do you?

ALEC: I do think she's very pretty, though.

LINDY: "Pretty?"

ALEC: Yes sir.

LINDY: "Pretty."

ALEC: I think she's easily the prettiest girl in town.

LINDY: And what about Wanda Jetvig? I thought she was the prettiest girl in town.

ALEC: Oh, Wanda's got nothing on Alison.

LINDY: You're putting me on.

ALEC: No sir, Lindy.

LINDY: What's the matter, Wanda's not your type?

ALEC: Wanda would be kind of pretty, I guess, if she got that look off her face. But I think Alison's prettier.

LINDY: That's not really very much to build a relationship on, though, is it?—thinking someone's pretty. Kind of an imma-ture way to get the ball rolling, if you ask me. When I met Cindy, I didn't think she was pretty at all, but I admired, very deeply, her mind.

ALEC: If I could go in, I'd get started at least—

LINDY: No, wait, tell me something else. If you think Alison's so pretty, Alec, why haven't you ever been out here to visit before? She's been here all summer long—

ALEC: I guess I figured she wasn't available.

LINDY: Why?

ALEC: Because of, uh, I don't know—

LINDY: Because of her big tummy?

ALEC: Yes sir.

LINDY: You're not really very committed, are you?

ALEC: Sir—

LINDY: You obviously must not think she's that pretty!

ALEC: Sir, why are you making this so hard for me?

LINDY: I don't know how many dates you've been on, Alec, but when a boy comes calling on a girl, the man of the house gets to do whatever he wants to the boy. That's nature's way. *(We hear the sound of glass breaking and then the sound of Cindy and Alison fighting fades in from offstage.)*

[ALISON: *(Offstage.)* That's what I think of your stupid old poodle skirt, you weirdo!]

[CINDY: Do you talk to your Mother this way?]

[ALISON: Do you set your daughters up with morticians?]

[CINDY: Oh, don't try that fancy logic on me, little lady, it won't work!]

(Another glass object is heard breaking offstage.)

LINDY: Do you think there's any chance you'll ever be leaving the funeral business, Alec?

ALEC: No sir.

LINDY: See, now, that's too bad. That's too bad for YOU. Because I'll be honest with you, Alec, Alison is a great girl. She's smart as a whip and she leads with her heart. And you're right, she IS the prettiest girl in this town; Wanda Jetvig oughta get that look off her face, you're a very perceptive young man.

ALEC: Thank you.

LINDY: So let me be straight with you again. My wife doesn't have any right getting involved in Alison's affairs. They're nobody's business but hers. And while you do seem like a decent young man, Alec, even if you were Spartacus, I don't think I could ever stand by and let Alison marry into your family, where breakfast, lunch and dinner are always right before a damn funeral!

ALEC: The decision is hers, though, right?

LINDY: *(Caught off guard.)* "Hers?" What do you mean?

ALEC: Well, like you said, sir, this is an affair of the heart, and it's nobody's business but hers. Like you said. Right?

LINDY: Of course. I mean, you're here, aren't you? I'm not about to throw you out. She is, but I'm not. By the way, did you see "Spartacus?"

ALEC: No sir.

LINDY: It's really a heck of a movie.

Scotland Road

Jeffrey Hatcher

2 Men—or—**Man & Woman**

John (30's-40's) a man searching for his future in the past, and Frances (80-90) sole survivor of the Titanic. **The role of Frances may be played by either a woman or a man.

Scene: a white room, the present

> *A young woman dressed in 19th century garb has been found clinging to an iceberg in the North Atlantic. When res-cued, she says only one word: Titanic. The mysterious and seemingly wealthy John has this strange woman brought to Maine where he and her Icelandic doctor attempt to discover the truth about her origins. When the last survivor of the world's most famous ship disaster is found to be living nearby, John brings the old lady to meet with their patient. Here, John meets with Frances for the first time and reveals some of his personal obsession with the Titanic disaster. (It should be noted that "Frances" is in actuality a man who saved himself by masquerading as a woman in order to board a lifeboat.*

○ ○ ○

John appears tense and nervous throughout.

JOHN: It was when I saw Telly Savalas fingering my great grand-mother's earrings…I knew then I had to dedicate myself to *preserving* the Titanic's sacred memory. The whole televised exhibition was violent in its disrespect. I stood transfixed before a television set. That bald man posturing there, some-where in France, as so-called "experts" in rented tuxedos and clip-on ties sat upon a stage under a tacky chandelier and smeared their fingers over the coins, the money-boxes, the silverware, the jewelry...all *ripped* from the cold, peaceful corpses' fingers. (Beat.)

MISS KITTLE: *(Deadpan.)* There weren't actually *corpses,* were there?

JOHN: Pardon-me?

MISS KITTLE: There weren't actually *corpses*, they didn't actually find *corpses*, there weren't really the remains of *corpses*? *(Beat.)*

JOHN: I was...speaking metaphorically.

MISS KITTLE: Yes, of course you were, dear. Will she be coming out soon?

JOHN: Yes! Dr. Halbrech just wants to make sure she's ready. Do you need anything?

MISS KITTLE: If I do, you can get my nurse on the other side of that door. Is it...*stuffy* in here?

JOHN: We...keep the temperature fairly *high*. I *should* tell you: in this place there are certain *words* we don't use in front of her.

MISS KITTLE: Words?

JOHN: Like..."air-conditioner." Words a woman from 1912 couldn't possibly have known. Trip-her-up sort of thing. We've managed to be pristine on this point. I'm sure you'll follow our lead.

MISS KITTLE: When Dr. Halbrech told me about the situation, I expected a very different...place. I expected a hospital. Or a sanitarium. A converted mansion, or one of those ghastly glass and steel things. But *this*...from the outside this looks so much...so much like a...

JOHN: Gas station.

MISS KITTLE: Yes.

JOHN: That's what it was. The cinderblock and the tank holes out front give it away. Abandoned years ago. It's perfect for this. Isolated, nothing around for miles, just the coast road and the sea. Room enough inside to build this room and her bedroom, connect the plumbing and pipes, space on the other side of this wall for monitors, a hot plate, a cot. *Heating* works rather well, don't you think? All done in less than a week.

MISS KITTLE: And you decided this was preferable to a hospital.

JOHN: Oh, she's perfectly taken care of here. Dr. Halbrech is a specialist in this area.

MISS KITTLE: *(Deadpan.)* Dr. Halbrech specializes in passengers of the Titanic?

JOHN: She's not being held against her will, she can leave anytime she likes. All she has to do is...*say.*

MISS KITTLE: And she hasn't.

JOHN: No. She hasn't.

MISS KITTLE: Do you expect me to recognize her?

JOHN: No, not at all, after eighty years, hardly. *She,* on the other hand, may *think* you *can.*

MISS KITTLE: Why?

JOHN: Well, you're *authentic. She's...* *(Uneasy pause. John takes paper from pocket.)* I, uh, I've prepared a list of questions for you to pose her. Specifics about...the night. I thought there might be some details you might not...that you might have—

MISS KITTLE: Forgotten?

JOHN: Well...if you find yourself at a loss, I'll be right there. *(He pockets the list.)* I'm surprised more people didn't try to seek you out. The "last living survivor of the Titanic." It's...quite a...*thrill. (Laughs nervously.)*

MISS KITTLE: There was a time when it wouldn't have been so strange to meet one. There were 705 of us. You just had to go to the right parties.

JOHN: But *you've* always lived in Maine, on the coast, in...seclusion.

MISS KITTLE: For eighty years.

JOHN: Never married?

MISS KITTLE: *(Deadpan.)* Not *so far.* I understand from Dr. Halbrech that you know quite a lot about the Titanic.

JOHN: I do, yes.

MISS KITTLE: Why? Other ships have been lost, after all. All the time.

JOHN: *(Increasingly agitated.)* The Titanic was different. The Titanic was the greatest ocean liner ever built, carrying aboard it the most glittering figures of it's day. The Titanic represented the bounds of modern society, for its achievements, for its glory, for its pride, for its arrogance—for a civilization creating a structure which could not help but drag its creators down to their deaths. The Titanic was a metaphor! *(Beat.)*

MISS KITTLE: *(Wry.)* Of course, we didn't think of it that way at the *time*.

JOHN: But...but the *stories*! Philadelphia millionaires playing bridge in the smoking lounge right through the end. Benjamin Guggenheim dressing in full evening clothes and opera cape. And my own great grandfather, John Jacob Astor, standing on the promenade deck with his faithful valet at his side as the ship plunged beneath the waves.

MISS KITTLE: *(Deadpan.)* Halcyon Days.

JOHN: Of course, there was great *shame* as well. The SS Californian that sat ten miles away and didn't lift a finger. The wireless operators who didn't send up the ice warnings fast enough. And, of course, the myth of the man who got off the ship dressed as a woman. At any rate, anything you can do that will make her...*uncomfortable*...make her *squirm*...well, that would be quite the thing.

MISS KITTLE: *(Staring at John.)* Oh, I enjoy watching people squirm.

JOHN: I should warn you: the woman...cries on occasion. Part of the performance, don't be alarmed. She cries at photographs of the real victims. A shoddy approximation of survivor guilt.

MISS KITTLE: What?

JOHN: Survivor guilt. It's common to...well...you would know better that I.

MISS KITTLE: Why?

JOHN: *(Nervously.)* Well...you're the last living survivor of the Titanic.

MISS KITTLE: (A nod to the bedroom.) Maybe not. I've never understood "survivor guilt." I lived, they died. Who's to say who's better off? One always makes a bargain to pay for the grace of God. But only if you can transform yourself. And whatever you transform yourself into, you must remain so forever. You define your future in the greatest moment of terror you have ever known. That which kept you *alive*...will be what you are for the rest of you life. (Pause.)

JOHN: Miss Kittle?

MISS KITTLE: Yes?

JOHN: Do you *dream* about the Titanic? (Beat.)

MISS KITTLE: No.

JOHN: Never?

MISS KITTLE: Mr. Astor, when I was picked up by the Carpathia the day after the sinking...I did not speak a word to a single soul. Not for days, not for weeks, not for months. And when we reached America, I returned to my family's home, went inside, closed the door, and I have not set foot outside its walls...until today. I don't *have* to *dream* about the Titanic. A dream is a name we give our thoughts. (Beat.) Do *you* dream, Mr. Astor? Of the Titanic?

JOHN: Yes.

MISS KITTLE: Do you dream you're on the Titanic? (Pause.)

JOHN: (Almost sad.) No. No, I don't dream I'm *on* the Titanic.

MISS KITTLE: But if you *had* been on the Titanic...what do you think you would have done?

JOHN: Behaved like a gentleman. Stood on the promenade deck, in the clear cold night...stood there in full evening clothes, as the ship slid beneath the waves.

MISS KITTLE: Alone? Why would anyone want to die alone? (John looks at Miss Kittle.) You're a very strange man, Mr. Astor. You're nostalgic for a disaster you never knew.

JOHN: We should start. (John moves to the bedroom door.)

MISS KITTLE: Mr. Astor: Don't be taken in by your dreams. There was more to the Titanic than the myth would have you believe. What you see, Mr. Astor, is just the tip.

Soda Fountain

Richard Lay

2 Men

Johnny (20's) a war hero, recently returned from Vietnam and Danny (20's) his best friend; a draft dodger.

Scene: a small American town. Summer, 1969

> When Johnny returns home from Vietnam a hero, he suspects that Sally, his fiancée, and Danny have been keeping company. Here the two young men share an uneasy reunion.

○ ○ ○

> Lights down and up. Johnny and Danny at opposite ends of stage...walk towards each other...pause, embrace, jock buddy buddy. Stand apart and study each other.

DANNY: *(Smiling.)* Kill many people?
JOHNNY: A few.
DANNY: How few's a few.
DANNY: More than you'd think.
> *(They look at each other—stand back and laugh like old friends. They hug again and sit on the ground. From a cooler Danny offers Johnny beer. He takes it. In silence they take four seconds for a swig—like who's going to speak again first.)*
DANNY: I'm glad you're back, old buddy.
JOHNNY: Sally tells me you managed to dodge that old Draft and have a picture of Jane Fonda over your bed. Is she sitting on a Commie tank or dressed up as Barbarella?
DANNY: C'mon Johnny. Look, I'm happy for you about the medal. You gonna get to meet Nixon?

JOHNNY: Matter of fact, next week...at the White House. A whole bunch of us.

DANNY: Whaddya want to do now...now you're back?

JOHNNY: Mainly nothing.

DANNY: *(Slightly anxious.)* I can understand that. I think I can understand that...but long term.

JOHNNY: Well, I got three years unspent pay...Oh, I don't know...Maybe shoot the breeze and drink beer at the Silver Bullet...have steak and eggs at The Fountain every morning...Play some pool *(Tension.)*...Do you still play pool, Danny?

DANNY: *(Pause.)* ...No.

JOHNNY: When I was in a fox-hole I used to imagine what my old buddy was doing. See, I always had it my mind's eye that you'd be planning some anti-war protest, volunteering to hand out blankets to the hippies and freaks and perhaps be shooting pool...perhaps with a soldier's girl friend.

DANNY: She told you, I guess...Well, there's nothing to it, Johnny. She told you we've been playing a little pool and drinking a few shots...The conversation was mainly about you. You know, when you were missing in action. She thought you was dead.

JOHNNY: She said beer.

DANNY: Shots, beer, what's the difference?

JOHNNY: The DIFFERENCE is that you don't buy other guys girl-friends shots, Danny, not unless you're planning a back-seat hi-jack. Remember, your own famous Sasparelli Spread eagle maneuver. What was it you used to say "Buy 'em a couple of shots—and you score a couple of shots."

DANNY: *(Slightly drunk.)* Come on Johnny, ease up. Sally and me are like brother and sister...Hey, warrior, you want to hit me for buying Sally a couple of drinks...Go right ahead. I even kissed her on the cheek a couple of times. Does that qualify me for a bullet in the head. Or maybe you'll creep up on me at night and slit my throat.

JOHNNY: *(Pause.)* Why did you say you don't play pool?

DANNY: Cos' I knew you'd get mad.

JOHNNY: You always knew how to get me mad, didn't you? Remember when we were scouts at summer camp and you collapsed my tent and I knew I hadn't got a clue how to put it up and it was dark and raining.

DANNY: That was your fault. You wouldn't share a tent! You had to bring your OWN tent.

JOHNNY: Then there was the time I was screwing Helen…and you were seeing her behind my back.

DANNY: All's fair in love and war and you were just better at the latter.

JOHNNY: *(Relaxing tension.)* Look, Danny, Nam is nearly over, I hope to God…I don't judge you or all the others who chose what you chose. I'm back and—and that's all I care about.

DANNY: How about Sally?

Soul Survivor
Ted Lange

2 Men
The Devil (any age) stealer of souls, and Guy (30's) an everyman
with a keen eye for detail.

Scene: here & now

> *Here, Old Scratch tries unsuccessfully to tempt Guy, a simple
> mailman with few earthly desires.*

○ ○ ○

GUY: What the hell?
DEVIL: Exactly.
GUY: How did you get in here?
DEVIL: Let's just say I was channeled.
    (The Devil turns off the T.V.)
GUY: Are you a repair man?
DEVIL: You might say I fix things.
GUY: Who told you to come here…the landlord?
DEVIL: No, the lord and I don't usually discuss my comings and
    goings.
GUY: Then who sent you?
DEVIL: You.
GUY: Me?
DEVIL: Uh-uh… *(He picks up a jar of Vaseline.)* You obviously have
    needs greasy man and I definitely have wants. I think we can
    do business.
    (The devil produces a business card.)
GUY: What the devil?
DEVIL: Exactamundo!
GUY: No more Jack Daniel's and pizza…
DEVIL: Or Vaseline.

GUY: You're the devil?

DEVIL: Very good. There are other names, but for now, that will do.

GUY: What do you want?

DEVIL: I want to buy your soul.

GUY: I gotta be dreaming.

DEVIL: Oh contraire. This is all quite real. I am offering to buy your soul...fair market value. I'll even throw in earthly benefits and we both can collect on our investments immediately.

GUY: You really want to buy my soul?

DEVIL: For all eternity.

GUY: Now let me get this straight...I sell my soul and what do I get?

DEVIL: Certainly more than this "Deep Throat Two, The Abyss." Why have it on tape when you can have the real thing?

GUY: Oh, sorry, you know how it is when you live alone.

DEVIL: Oh, yes!

GUY: What's all this about fair market value, earthly benefits? What do you mean?

DEVIL: I mean, I get your soul and you get whatever you want. Name it.

(Guy picks up a photograph of his old girlfriend.)

GUY: Hmmmm. How about true love? I sell my soul and you give me true love.

DEVIL: True love is a little too saccharine for my taste. How 'bout I give you the most beautiful woman in the world—how's that?

GUY: No, no, no. Too many inherent problems. Other men hitting on her. Other woman doing the same. I'm looking for a woman with integrity. Honesty. Likes me for who I am. Won't lie to me. Somebody I can trust and someone who trusts me. You know, true love.

DEVIL: Titty's—how about big titty's? Forty-two double "D" cup. Pretty face. Nice big legs. Black guys love big legs. Plus she'll screw your brains out. How about that?

GUY: Sounds good, but...

DEVIL: Okay, okay, okay. How about money? What if I give you a million dollars? I'm talking cash. Right now, one million dollars. All yours.

GUY: How would I explain that to the IRS?

DEVIL: Say it was a gift.

GUY: But I'll be taxed.

DEVIL: So?

GUY: So, wouldn't quite end up a million. I don't get it all. That's like the lottery. Why don't you give me the ability to make money.

DEVIL: You must be crazy? I'm gonna give you one million dollars for one lousy soul and you don't want to take it.

GUY: Oh, I want to take it. But I want to be able to keep it.

DEVIL: *(To himself.)* Oh, I got a tough one here.

GUY: Got anything else? Maybe we just haven't hit on the right thing.

(He takes the pocket computer.)

DEVIL: Yeah. Let's see—AIDS, avarice, anathema, action comic books, Nah! "B", "C", "D", "E". Oh, here, how about being famous? I'll make you famous then it will be easier for you to find true love. Kind of a two-for-one sale.

GUY: You're not very creative? Don't you think I read the National Enquirer? One good dose of fame and I'm naked in a rain storm. No more privacy. Paparazzi in the bathroom. Groupies at the Laundromat. Fanatics following me; maybe even stalking me. Hey, for no reason, I might get shot just because I got a little fame.

DEVIL: Yeah, but you'll always be able to get a good table at a fancy restaurant.

GUY: There must be more to life than eating.

DEVIL: Not really. Speaking of which, fame will help you get free poontang.

GUY: Now we're back to my first request. What I really want. True love.

DEVIL: I said free poontang. Not true love.

GUY: What's the difference?

216 men's scenes

DEVIL: Free poontang is a woman with no strings attached. She's all yours for a night. You don't even have to see her again. She'll suck your toes, lick your fingers, kiss you. She'll cream and steam you. Do everything but redeem you. Won't talk too much. Won't ask embarrassing questions, won't take your money. Tell her to go? She's gone. Don't even have to remember her name. You get to go about your life as you like and once in a while throughout the course of your travels— free poontang drops in. Wet and warm. Seductive and sensual. And you can do whatever you want with it. Give her to a friend or keep her for yourself. She's free. She's yours. The All-American Dream. Free Poontang.

GUY: Is it clean?

DEVIL: What? What cha mean—clean?

GUY: You know, clean. No disease. No Crabs. No little creepy, crawly things running in and out of that free poontang. You know clean!

DEVIL: Jesus Christ! I mean hell and damnation, you just ruined one of my favorite sales pitches with this "clean shit?"

GUY: The least you can do is guarantee the quality of the merchandise.

DEVIL: I have given that pitch to millions of souls. Never have I been so insulted with—is it clean?

GUY: Maybe you weren't going after good quality souls.

DEVIL: I'll be the judge of that.
(Hellish effect.)

GUY: Why don't you just pass on me?

DEVIL: Ah, forgive me. Sometimes I get a little irritable. You know, heart burn.
(The Devil laughs, Guy doesn't.)

DEVIL: You intrigue me. Let's think about this. *(Pause.)* If a man could have his fondest wish—what would it be?

GUY: I don't know.

DEVIL: Don't rush. I said let's think about this. We tried women. How about men?
(Guy shakes his head no.)

GUY: Not my style.

DEVIL: I didn't think so. Just checking. How about an incredibly satisfying job?

GUY: Actually, I love my work.

DEVIL: Working for the Post Office?

GUY: Yeah. Great, huh?

DEVIL: Don't get me wrong, I don't mean to offend you— but nobody likes working for the Post Office.

GUY: I do.

DEVIL: It's a crappy job. I know, I invented it. As a penance.

GUY: Well, I love it. I'd rather be a postman than a bartender… stuck behind some crummy bar…on a boat. I get to walk all over the city. Out and about, sharing life with nature. Bird watching. People watching.

DEVIL: I don't believe this?

GUY: Plus, I'm really good at my job. I satisfy a lot of people. Hey, if I don't show up on the first and fifteenth, a lot of welfare mothers would be upset. But I'm always there. Sometimes they're so glad to see me, they greet me with cookies and milk.

DEVIL: This is sickening.

GUY: And during tax return time, I'm the most popular guy in the neighborhood. I come through with the mail, no matter what.

DEVIL: I know, through rain and shit.

GUY: Sleet. Rain and sleet.

DEVIL: This would be so much easier if you were only greedy.

GUY: Look who wants thing easier? My daddy taught me, you measure the quality of your life by how hard you work for it.

DEVIL: Okay, okay. Let me think. I offered fame, fortune, and for-nication. Guess that leaves only my ace. And I hate to play my ace, but under the circumstances…I do have my reputation to think about.

GUY: What reputation?

DEVIL: Well, I can't go around offering to buy souls and then get turned down. If this sort of thing ever gets back to God, it sort of proves his point.

GUY: What's God's point?

DEVIL: Oh, you know, "Purity of Heart," "Goodness of Soul," "Faith." "Kingdom of Heaven." All that stuff.

GUY: "Kingdom of Heaven." I've always wondered about that.

DEVIL: Wondered about what?

GUY: If you have to be a member of a certain religion to get into the Kingdom Of Heaven.

DEVIL: Like a country club? Ha-ha-ha-ha-ha-ha-ha-ha-ha-ha-ha-ha. Hell no!

GUY: You mean you can get in without being a Christian, or Jew, or Moslem, or Buddhist?

DEVIL: Ha-ha-ha-ha-ha-ha-ha-ha-ha-ha-ha-ha. Hell yes!

GUY: Are you sure? I thought you had to belong to a church?

DEVIL: Hell, you can be an atheist and still get in. You just have to live an exemplary life. The church thing was something I started.

GUY: You?

DEVIL: Yeah. *(Modest but proud.)* Actually, quite ingenious little plan if I must say so myself. There was sort of a lull in my membership department. So I had to do something. I needed to get everyone to think they'll get closer to God by talking to an intermediary who says he's got the direct connection to God. Then have the intermediary set up business in what he calls God's house—church. Then have everybody go to God's house to find God instead of looking for Him in themselves. That gives me more time to contaminate their minds and get their little souls. Sheer genius!

GUY: So, we don't really need...say...a priest?

DEVIL: Nope.

GUY: Rabbi?

DEVIL: Uh-uh.

GUY: Allah, God, Jehovah? Aren't they different Gods?

DEVIL: No. Negatory.

GUY: Wow!

DEVIL: Who did the non Christian American Indians worship? Or the Australian Aborigines. The Zulu's of Africa, the Samoans. Hell, those guys were around long before the missionaries. If you just followed the Ten Commandments, you'd be doing everything you need to get into heaven. Life is no more complicated than that. Stray from the top ten and you're raking leaves in my garden.

GUY: Simple.

DEVIL: Yeah, too simple that's why I had to mess with that. God makes it too easy, so I threw in a little subterfuge. I came up with a little thing called "Confession." Now listen to this, it's a beauty.

GUY: I know what a confession is.

DEVIL: No, you don't. You just think you know. You go to church, do a lot of genuflecting, then you sit in a booth and confess to sins you have committed. Transgressions. Some guy who went to school to study religion, and got a "C" plus average is listening to your story. Your sins. Then this guy tells you to do a couple of Hail Mary's. God forgives you and your slate is clean with God. You get up, go out feeling really good, 'till you're confronted with chance to sin again which I arrange. So you sin. A good solid, no holds barred gimme all you got "sin." You go back to Father "C" plus. He absolves you of this sin too. Hey! You're on a roll. Now you know you can sin and sin and still be absolved as long as you confess. No matter how big the sin is, just tell old "C" plus exactly what went on and you're off the hook. Brilliant, huh?

GUY: No, not really. Because God forgives you.

DEVIL: Here's the real beauty of it. Just once!

GUY: Just once?

DEVIL: Yeah, God forgives you just once. And that's it, buddy. Over and out.

GUY: You mean, you can't be absolved of a sin more than once? *(The Devil sits on a stool.)*

DEVIL: Hell no. What, you think God is a fool? He knows what's happening. Everybody just goes on committing sins, and the

"C" plus priest is saying their slate is clean; meanwhile, I'm racking up points every time a soul falters.

GUY: And you made this up?

DEVIL: Yes, indeed. I came up with the idea, designed the format, and implemented the structure. Which brings me to my favorite offer to particularly stubborn souls.

GUY: Is it an offer I can't refuse?

DEVIL: I don't think you can.

GUY: Have you used this pitch on many people?

DEVIL: No, I try to save it for particularly tough cases.

GUY: I'm a tough case?

DEVIL: Yeah. Kind of a hard sell.

GUY: Can you give me an example of an easy sale?

DEVIL: You mean name names?

GUY: Yeah.

DEVIL: That's bad form. I kind of like to keep my client list confidential.

GUY: Well then, how would I know if you've really had satisfied customers?

DEVIL: Trust me. *(Pause.)* Okay, I'll give you a name.

GUY: Not Robert Johnson. I'm not into the Blues.

DEVIL: How about Hitler?

GUY: Oh, sure. Give a name everybody knows. Why didn't you say Atilla the Hun or Lecretia Borsia. Everybody knows Hitler was a client of yours. I'm asking for a name people might not readily know, and I can then look at the quality of that person's life and make a judgment if I want to sell.

DEVIL: Yeah, yeah, yeah. I can do that. How about Burton?

GUY: Levar Burton?

DEVIL: No, Richard Burton.

GUY: Richard Burton, the actor?

DEVIL: No, Richard Burton, the left handed gynecologist. Of course, I mean Richard Burton, the actor.

(The Devil starts to exit to the kitchen.)

GUY: Wait, wait, wait. You bought Richard Burton's soul?

DEVIL: Are you kidding? He couldn't wait to sell. But that's typical of most actors. Usually you don't have to offer them much more than fame and they're ready to bite.

GUY: I don't believe you.

DEVIL: Why would I lie?

GUY: 'Cause you're the devil.

DEVIL: I'll prove it.

(The Devil stamps three times and yells down to the floor.)

DEVIL: Hey Richie, sing us a song.

(Burton's voice can be heard singing "Camelot.")

GUY: That's him. That's definitely him.

(The Devil lets the song go on for awhile.)

DEVIL: I could have given him a better singing voice, but he was more interested in a used vagina.

GUY: You mean Liz?

DEVIL: Liz. Pretty good deal, huh? Remember when he did the play *Dr. Faustus*? He was recreating our first meeting.

GUY: Liz.

DEVIL: Sure. He was hoping I'd come back so he could adjust the contract. A very moving performance, but a deal's a deal.

GUY: I don't think he made out so well?

DEVIL: What? Are you kidding? He did great. He had fame, fortune, and the most beautiful woman in the world.

GUY: But didn't they get divorced?

DEVIL: Twice.

GUY: And wasn't he an alcoholic?

DEVIL: He drank a little.

GUY: And as an actor, he never won an Academy Award.

DEVIL: He didn't ask for one. I would have given him one if he'd ask. I gave Cher hers.

GUY: Cher? You gave Cher…

DEVIL: Cher, Whoopie Goldberg, Quentin Tarantino. Hey, surely you don't think Cher got the Oscar for that performance. Up against Glenn Close, give me a break. That took some doing, and I must say I had to do a lot of finessing. I had to fuck…but it worked. I always keep my bargains, as you will soon find out.

222 men's scenes

GUY: I don't want to be another Richard Burton.

DEVIL: He had a great life. Money, fame, and Liz.

GUY: Yeah, but what did he do with his money? He never produced a great movie or play with it. Never hired writers to write decent parts for himself.

DEVIL: True, Olivier will be remembered for the great roles.

GUY: And the little I've read about his wife, well, that couldn't have been any picnic.

DEVIL: Well that's true. She did get fat as a pig. On and off pills. Drank like a fish and didn't respect him in public. But that's life in the fast lane. Every turn an adventure.

GUY: If I make a deal with you, I want to know I'm going to be happy with a loving wife, healthy children, a good job, and some time to go fishing.

DEVIL: Fishing? Get a life. Carpe Diem! "Seize the day." I give you my final offer. My ace. The best of the bunch. Here it is... Power.

GUY: Power? What kind of power?

DEVIL: Any kind of power. Power over men. Power over women. Power to give power. Power to take power. Power over the mind. Your mind. Their mind. Any mind.

GUY: I think I've heard enough.

DEVIL: No, you haven't. I'm in the middle of the pitch. Power to kill. Good, huh? Power to change lives. Power to inspire. Power to walk into a room and generate fear. The biggest man will cower. The brightest will defer. Think it. Presidents and kings seeking you out. Women worshipping you. People recognizing you as a man of power. And all of them kissing your power filled ass.

GUY: This is a terrible mistake.

DEVIL: Don't tell me you don't want power.

GUY: No, not really.

DEVIL: Even housewives in Peoria want power.

GUY: Well, not me.

DEVIL: I don't believe you. Every man has his price. You're just trying to stress me out.

(Hellish effect.)

GUY: I'm ready to sell, but, you're just not making the right offers. I told you what I want.

DEVIL: Not back to this true love shit.

GUY: Give me a break, will ya. What in the world am I gonna do with power?

DEVIL: Rule the world.

GUY: That's a lot of responsibility. I just want to have a fulfilling live, knowing that I can go to work, do my job the best that it can be done, watch my children grow and learn, and make life a little fun for my friends.

DEVIL: "Make life a little fun for your friends!"

GUY: I don't understand why you can find me a woman, but not my true love.

DEVIL: Because I can't.

DEVIL & GUY: Jesus.

DEVIL: There's someone I really miss. Like you, he was a challenge. A real goody two sandals.

GUY: Did you try to tempt Jesus?

DEVIL: Boy, you want to talk about purity of soul. If I could have got His soul, I wouldn't need all those crappy little souls I'm getting now. The brimstone of my kingdom would shine so bright, you would have thought it was a Super Nova. Can you imagine His soul being consumed in Hell? Wow!! Gives me the chills.

GUY: But you didn't get Him?

DEVIL: Almost did. Got Him to draw up a contract and everything…

GUY: And?

DEVIL: He got me in the fine print. Always got to look out for that fine print.

GUY: What did the fine print say?

DEVIL: That he had me for all eternity, instead of me having him for…oh no you don't. Very clever, 'lil prick.

GUY: What?

DEVIL: Getting me to reminisce and take my mind off business.

224 men's scenes

GUY: I was just curious.

DEVIL: Curious?

GUY: Yeah. But I think I understand now.

DEVIL: Understand what?

GUY: That it's true.

DEVIL: What's true?

GUY: The after life. It's real. It exists.

DEVIL: Of course it exists. How do you think I got here?

GUY: Exactly, that's my point. Up until now, you were just a myth to me. A legend. A spooky story designed to frighten somebody into leading a good life—with no guarantees of what's on the other side or meeting God.

DEVIL: You mean 'cause I showed up you now believe in God?

GUY: Oh, I've always believed in God. But I had no proof. I often felt His presence. Couldn't see Him. Couldn't touch Him.

DEVIL: I'm living proof that He exists?

GUY: Exactly and that means Jesus lived and He truly was the Son of God. And I should not fear the unknown because it really is known.

DEVIL: You used me to confirm your belief in God?

GUY: Yes.

DEVIL: Ain't that a bitch.

GUY: Thank you.

DEVIL: Don't thank me. You know, I got cards I haven't played yet. The Dream Sequence.

GUY: What is the Dream Sequence?

DEVIL: That's the one when you're not sure this really happened—everything seems real, but was it real?

GUY: Like an acid trip?

DEVIL: An acid trip you know—this you won't.

GUY: Yadda, yadda, yadda, yadda.

DEVIL: You know, you're a smart little asshole and capturing your soul is going to be a pleasure.
(Hellish effect.)

GUY: The more I think about it, the more I think I'll keep my soul. You can go now.

DEVIL: Well, I'm not gonna let you go. It took a lot of effort for me to get here. I'm not returning home empty handed.

GUY: You made your offers and I declined.

DEVIL: Ah, yes, but the game is just beginning. You see—I understand that a quality soul takes time. And I got eternity. I'm gonna reel you in like a flounder.

GUY: I thought you thought fishing was boring?

DEVIL: Depends on the fish.

GUY: I told you I ain't biting.

DEVIL: Oh, you'll bite. You can bet your little black booty on this one.

(The Guy goes to the front door, stops, and turns. The Devil tosses Guy an apple from a basket of fruit. Guy catches the apple and looks at it.)

GUY: No, thanks. I'm a Wheaties man.

(Guy tosses the apple back. The Devil catches it. Then Guy exits. The Devil stomps on the floor three times.

DEVIL: Richie, give us a song, will ya.

(Richard Burton's voice starts to sing "I Wonder What The King Is Doing Tonight." Blackout.)

subCITY

Bob Jude Ferrante

2 Men

Father Conan (60) a Jesuit priest; smart, literate and secretly gay,
and Wall (20's) a seminary student, gay.

Scene: St. Agatha's, a Catholic parish in Danbury, CT

*When Wall requests a letter of recommendation for the
priesthood from Father Conan, the older man refuses. Here,
Wall confronts his mentor and forces him to reveal his reasons.*

○ ○ ○

*Lights. Father Conan at his office desk at St. Agatha's—a
200-year-old Catholic parish in Danbury, Connecticut. Father
Conan looks through papers; draws a handkerchief out and
wipes his face; stuffs the handkerchief back in his pocket
without looking up once. Silence.*

FATHER CONAN: Metempsychosis. *(Looks in dictionary.)*
Metempsychosis. Metempsychosis. Huh. "The transmigration
of souls; the journey of the spirit through the ether…" *(A
knock.)* Come in.
*(Wall trips over something in the crowded office, a thump.
Father Conan does not look up.)*
FATHER CONAN: Softly.
*(Silence. Wall enters. Father Conan holds up his hand for a
moment. Wall waits. Wall sits. Beat, then Father Conan looks
up quickly, serious-faced.)*
FATHER CONAN: Ah. Wall.
WALL: You wanted to see me, Monsignor Conan?
FATHER CONAN: *(Looks down on his desk for a file, does not look
up.)* Yes. *(Beat. Finally he looks at Wall.)* I told Charlie to put

the clippings on my desk. How am I supposed to do a homily on the Challenger tragedy without any facts? Oh, Charlie. Charlie. So young, so promising, so...clueless. *(Pause.)* I guess it would be a cliché if I said you can't get good help any more? *(Pause. Wall fidgets, uncomfortable.)* How am I to appear omniscient without *clippings? (Laughs to himself.)* The flock doesn't want to know we're human, They demand gold lavers and spectacle, but drop fifty cents into the collection plate to do it on.

WALL: Sir?

FATHER CONAN: Sorry. Mother Superior would say I need a good night's sleep.

WALL: I can come back. *(Beat.)*

FATHER CONAN: Wall, that was quite impressive.

WALL: Really?

FATHER CONAN: "Really?" Such understatement. It was Emersonian... *(Drifting.)* "Born for success he seemed / with grace to win, with heart to hold / with shining gifts that took all eyes..." *(Finds a folder and holds it up.)* Your request for a letter of recommendation for the priesthood.

WALL: You need me to tell you what to say?

FATHER CONAN: I want to say...first, how proud...You're bright of the bright. Brightest. With echoing words from Father Hayman in English. Which one would figure, English is your forte. Under normal circumstances a student with your record who makes a request like goes..."onward and..." *(With a hand, gestures upward.)*

WALL: I'm looking forward to it.
(Beat.)

FATHER CONAN: Under normal circumstances.
(Silence.)

WALL: So, circumstances are not normal.

FATHER CONAN: Bright and perceptive beyond your years. Though the two go hand-in-hand, I would assume.

WALL: But, you can't write the letter?

FATHER CONAN: It's more than that. I am your adviser. No matter what the others think or say, I cast the final vote whether you get in or not.

WALL: And you vote, "no."

FATHER CONAN: I'll let you in on a little dilemma. You tell me what you would do in my position. *(Slight pause.)* Let's pretend there's this small Catholic school. The student body is mostly knuckleheads, any one of whom is fully capable of murdering their own grandmother for the price of a pint of wine.

WALL: In other words, Saint Agatha's.

FATHER CONAN: Right. And you are a mid-level administrator responsible for seven classes full of the aforementioned knuckleheads.

WALL: In other words, you.

FATHER CONAN: Right. One day, a lay fellow is assigned to your late afternoon class. He lights up the room He can spot a "nine" stuffed in a back pocket. He's gay.

WALL: In other words, me.

FATHER CONAN: Other people can hide it. You could ask him to hide it better. But it's not his nature.

WALL: I won't embarrass you.

FATHER CONAN: How much this must hurt, to think that of me! If it were only embarrassment, there would be no issue. We need to think of the flock. They are impressionable. They need the right example set. What if there were nocturnal visits? Overnight guests. Would that be a good example?

WALL: There wouldn't be.

FATHER CONAN: The Jesuit priesthood is no "profession!" It is a calling. From God. To fulfill its duties, you must give of yourself, to the point of ultimate sacrifice. The oaths…poverty. Humility. Celibacy…

WALL: I can do that.

FATHER CONAN: "Damian's…Treehouse?"

WALL: That was *once*.

FATHER CONAN: This is *Danbury*. Not…New York City or something. A *Celibate* merely avoids sexual congress with *women*. A *Jesuit* applies stricter rules. *(Pause.)* And the flock. The

example you set. *(Pause.)* A weaker soul. A weaker soul would… would rubber-stamp this and look away. Feeling would cloud better judgment. If I let you pass and there were…damage done… no man would blame *me*. But for Jesuits, the call possesses the heart and you are forced to act. *(Wall puts his head down. Father Conan speaks even more gently, lays his hand on Wall's shoulder.)* What you must do is go back and think on your life. You are at an important juncture. *(Beat.)* There is an alternative to the priesthood. I talked to Brother Dewey. He says there's room.
(Pause.)

WALL: The Gregorians.

FATHER CONAN: Have you seen their campus? A garden. A fortress. A great mind must be sheltered. Acquinas said…

WALL: I don't want to know what Acquinas said. I want you to do the right thing by me.

FATHER CONAN: You may not be able to see it today, but by turning you down, I do you a favor.

WALL: A favor! *(Stands to leave.)*

FATHER CONAN: Think about it, Wall. You belong in a life of contemplation. I can see you in twenty years…published…a voice to rival Muggeridge. Merton.

WALL: *(Sarcastically.)* Acquinas. *(Pause.)* I could mention… *(Beat; he leans closer.)* That day in the nave…next to the Saint Anthony…

FATHER CONAN: *(Explodes.)* That's *precisely* what I am talking about! You are putting your own needs before that of the flock. Suppose you spoke out about our moment of weakness and I lost my calling? Where would the flock be?

WALL: Oh. The flock.

FATHER CONAN: Until you can put their needs before yours, you will never be a priest. *(Pause.)*

WALL: Gather Conan, thanks to your conscience and heart, I will never be one anyway.
(He exits. Father Conan stands, starts to stop him, then relents and lets him go. Pause. He draws a handkerchief out and wipes his face. Darkness.)

When Cuba Opens Up

Benjie Aerenson

3 Men

Wayne and Timmy (50's) small-time burglars, and Johnny (20's) a small-time thief.

Scene: an efficiency apartment in Miami

> *Johnny wants to rob a house and here does his best to enlist Wayne and Timmy.*

O O O

> *In the efficiency apartment on motel row in Miami beach where Wayne and Timmy are living; Johnny is there.*

TIMMY: You know that movie

WAYNE: What movie

TIMMY: That movie, you know the one.

WAYNE: No I don't know the one and it really pisses me off you say that movie and expect me to know the one

TIMMY: The movie with the horse

WAYNE: There's plenty movies with horses

TIMMY: The old one where they put on the masks and knock over the race track

JOHNNY: Are you guys gonna listen to what I have to say

WAYNE: *(To Timmy.)* Yeah right "The Killers" so what about it

TIMMY: So you know the damn thing's going to go wrong

WAYNE: Why

TIMMY: They shoot the horse

WAYNE: So big deal they shoot the horse to create a distraction

TIMMY: The horse isn't involved

JOHNNY: What are you guys talking about

WAYNE: He is involved

JOHNNY: He's a horse

WAYNE: He's a race horse. I can see if he's some horse out somewhere grazing in the woods

JOHNNY: Horses don't graze in the woods

WAYNE: The hell they don't

JOHNNY: They graze in pastures

WAYNE: Pastures woods whatever if he's eating the fucking grass
I can see okay, but he's not. He's a race horse and he's racing
at the track. And he's not racing at just any track, he's racing
at the track they're hitting. So he's involved.

(Pause.)

TIMMY: Okay.

(Pause.)

JOHNNY: Yeah he's right it's like a dog at a house you hit, they say
oh they killed the poor dog, but the dog was involved

(Pause.)

TIMMY: You kill dogs?

JOHNNY: Are you guys gonna hear me out

TIMMY: I want to know about this dog

JOHNNY: I didn't say I killed dogs

TIMMY: Do you

JOHNNY: No

(Pause.)

TIMMY: Wayne killed the fucking cat

WAYNE: The cat was sick. We put him down

TIMMY: I didn't want to. You made me

WAYNE: We went together

TIMMY: You talked me into it. Why did I let you talk me into it

WAYNE: He was old and suffering

TIMMY: He wasn't suffering. He was old but he wasn't suffering

WAYNE: He was losing weight. He had no hair. How could you
stand to look at him

TIMMY: That's why he killed the cat, 'cause it scared him to look
at him, 'cause it scares him to get old

WAYNE: You're full of shit

TIMMY: I'll regret that till the day I die, I'll never get over that

JOHNNY: Are you guys gonna—

WAYNE: Then you shouldn't've gotten swayed, you should've stood up for yourself, he doesn't stand up

TIMMY: That's the last time, I'm never letting you talk me into anything

JOHNNY: What about this proposition.

TIMMY: Sonofabitch

(Pause.)

WAYNE: Look at him. He broods. He gets quiet. He draws into himself

JOHNNY: Are we gonna talk about this

WAYNE: But now it's all better. He got it off his chest.

TIMMY: It's still on my chest

WAYNE: Fuck you

JOHNNY: Are we gonna talk about—

WAYNE: Let's go get something to eat and talk about it

TIMMY: I don't feel like talking about it

WAYNE: We'll go to Rascal House

TIMMY: I said I don't want to talk about it.

(Pause.)

WAYNE: There's worse things that happen

TIMMY: Worse than what

WAYNE: Worse than the cat. What about that guy who walks into the Wreck Bar and shoots the parrot

TIMMY: What about him

WAYNE: That was for no reason. Who the hell shoots a parrot for no reason

TIMMY: What reason is there ever to shoot a parrot

WAYNE: Exactly what I'm saying. That's pure meanness

JOHNNY: Some places they eat them

TIMMY: Nobody eats parrots

JOHNNY: In the jungle they do

TIMMY: Nobody eats anything that beautiful

JOHNNY: They do where there's nothing less beautiful to eat

(Pause.)

TIMMY: The line will be too long

WAYNE: Huh
TIMMY: At Rascal House
WAYNE: Not at this time of day
JOHNNY: Who cares where we go
WAYNE: The food's good at Rascal House
TIMMY: It's fresh
WAYNE: I said it's good
TIMMY: It's good because it's fresh
WAYNE: Okay alright
TIMMY: Not because it's made good but because it's fresh
WAYNE: It's made good too
TIMMY: I didn't say it wasn't
    (Johnny opens and closes a drawer repeatedly, slamming it closed very hard each time to get their attention. He leaves it bounced open a bit.)
    (Pause.)
WAYNE: You're gonna break that drawer.
TIMMY: I don't think I'm in
WAYNE: What
TIMMY: You heard me
WAYNE: Listen to what he's got to say
TIMMY: I'm thinking about making a change
WAYNE: A what
TIMMY: A change. My nerves
JOHNNY: I'll see you later
WAYNE: Relax, he's just upset about the cat
TIMMY: It's more than that. I'm getting too jumpy being in places I'm not supposed to be
JOHNNY: I don't need this
WAYNE: I told you he's okay
TIMMY: I'm a bundle of nerves, I can't stand it anymore.
WAYNE: This is a quick in and out
TIMMY: And all day long I'm sick to my stomach. I need something less stressful
JOHNNY: Are you kidding or are you negotiating
TIMMY: I was thinking I could be a poolboy

234 men's scenes

(Pause.)
JOHNNY: He's serious
WAYNE: You're over fifty years old
TIMMY: Poolman
WAYNE: And aren't you forgetting something
TIMMY: What
WAYNE: You can't swim
TIMMY: I didn't say I wanted to be a lifeguard, I said I wanted to be a poolboy
JOHNNY: He doesn't swim?
WAYNE: He doesn't
TIMMY: Wayne doesn't either
WAYNE: I swim, I just don't go swimming
TIMMY: Same thing
WAYNE: The hell it is.
TIMMY: You live on the beach and you haven't been in the ocean in twenty years
WAYNE: The ocean's for tourists
(Johnny takes a shaving brush out of the still slightly open drawer.)
JOHNNY: You shave with a brush?
TIMMY: What are you doing with that
JOHNNY: My old man shaved with a brush, I didn't think anybody else did
TIMMY: I do. Put it back
JOHNNY: You keep it in the drawer
TIMMY: I switch off
WAYNE: He lets that one rest
TIMMY: Wayne
JOHNNY: Is it some kind of pet
TIMMY: Put it down
(Johnny puts it down.)
(Pause.)
JOHNNY: They're going to be at the Heat game
TIMMY: Who
JOHNNY: The people who own this house

TIMMY: I told you I' m not…

WAYNE: You're a thief, Timmy, you're not a swimmer. Try to be what you are, stick to what you know

JOHNNY: Wayne's right. I was reading this article it said it's all in the genes all what you're gonna do

TIMMY: I don't believe it

WAYNE: It's a fact. They found the genes for it, a thief, a killer. And the thing is, you got to be the best you can at whatever you're meant to do

JOHNNY: That's where things go wrong, like when a burglar tries to pull an armed job and somebody gets hurt because he's not sticking to what he's meant to do
(Pause.)

TIMMY: How do you know what you're meant to do

WAYNE: It feels right…

TIMMY: Nothing feels right

WAYNE: Your genes are constipated
(Johnny heads for the door.)

JOHNNY: I'll shop this down the beach

WAYNE: The fuck you will, just relax

JOHNNY: I got a poolboy and…

WAYNE: I told you he's not going to be a poolboy. (To Timmy.) Just listen to what the kid has to say

JOHNNY: The Heat are playing the Magic

TIMMY: So

JOHNNY: So these homeowners will be at the game and a back window will be open

TIMMY: How do you know

JOHNNY: I know. And we'll be able to watch them while we're in their house.

TIMMY: How are we going to watch 'em if we're in their house and they're at the game

JOHNNY: 'Cause they sit on the floor. They got season tickets on the floor.

TIMMY: On the floor?

JOHNNY: Right down on it

TIMMY: You think it's so good to sit on the floor at the Heat games

JOHNNY: I don't give a fuck what it's good to do, all I'm tellin' you is…

TIMMY: I wouldn't give you a nickel for it, everybody standing up, the Coaches, the press

WAYNE: Listen to this guy, he never got near the floor and he's tellin' you how it is

TIMMY: I can see how it is on TV, these guys think they're big shots sitting on the floor, and you know what the players think of them, they think who are these assholes getting in my way, I'm dripping sweat all over them and they're smiling. I couldn't give a shit about them
(Pause.)

WAYNE: Wait till we're on the floor and then say that

TIMMY: I wouldn't take tickets on the floor if you gave them to me

WAYNE: The hell

TIMMY: the Heat the Heat, basketball football speedboats, they got no culture down here

WAYNE: It's too pretty for culture

TIMMY: It's

WAYNE: Culture is something you do on a rainy day, when you can't go outside for recess. Down here it's too nice for culture. Up north they do things inside because they got no life outside. Down here even going out to the mailbox is a beautiful thing, the green lizards in the planter, the snails on the striped leaves, the sun on the hibiscus. But up north by the time you walk down four flights to get your mail, if the mailbox was an oven you'd stick your head in it. I hate it up there, the quality of life is zip. Of course, down here you can't keep people inside long enough to take anything seriously
(Johnny lifts the end of the bed and starts slamming it up and down against the floor.)

TIMMY: You're going to upset the fucking neighbors

JOHNNY: You're…the both of… We'll come in through the back

men's scenes 237

window, we'll turn on the TV, no sound, to the Heat game, every time the camera shoots the Heat bench, we'll be able to keep an eye on them

WAYNE: Who are these people

JOHNNY: People with tickets to the Heat and a ten thousand square foot house

WAYNE: How do you know what they look like

JOHNNY: I got their picture

WAYNE: Let's see

JOHNNY: Not with me

TIMMY: The kid doesn't have their picture, the kid doesn't know what he's talking about

JOHNNY: I told you I've got it, just not with me
(Pause.)

TIMMY: Go on, Wayne, do what you want to do. I'll stay here

WAYNE: You're not going to be a poolboy

TIMMY: I was thinking about it

WAYNE: You won't be able to keep your hands out of their pockets when they're taking a swim

TIMMY: I can

WAYNE: You can't. Every job he ever had something was missing. Something will be missing from their lounge chair while they're doing the breaststroke

TIMMY: It'll be different

JOHNNY: It's all or none

WAYNE: *(To Johnny.)* Just give me a chance here

TIMMY: And what about the hawk

JOHNNY: What hawk

TIMMY: The hawk that fixed my eye through the Courthouse window, when I was on the twelfth floor of the Courthouse getting probation

WAYNE: If that hawk picked up your cat and carried it away you wouldn't be talking like that

TIMMY: What does one thing have to do with another

WAYNE: It looks at you so you think it's your friend

TIMMY: I didn't say it was my friend, I said it made eye contact

238 men's scenes

WAYNE: It was there for the pigeons

TIMMY: It looked at me, it was flying through the sky outside the Courthouse window and it stopped and hovered and fixed my eye, when a wild animal makes eye contact with you it means something

JOHNNY: What did you do next

TIMMY: I didn't know what to do, that's the point, I knew it meant something but I didn't know what
(Pause.)

TIMMY: I think if I lived a different kind of life I'd know what these things meant

WAYNE: What kind of life

TIMMY: One that you could look straight out through all you do into the eyes of a wild animal

JOHNNY: What the fuck's he talking about

WAYNE: Except you're a thief, Timmy, your life is based upon lying and deception, your every move is deception, is a lie, is being someplace you're not supposed to be. You can't look in anyone's eyes because you act while their head is turned

TIMMY: That's why I can't keep doing it

WAYNE: If you wanted to stop you'd just do it and stop talking about it. As long as Timmy's talking I know he's not going anywhere
(Pause.)

WAYNE: Forget breakfast at the Rascal House, you can forget that. You won't even have enough to take yourself out to breakfast

TIMMY: I'll be alright

WAYNE: I see the geezers, buying food for a week's worth of breakfast, you know what, they ask me to snap the carton of a dozen eggs in half. They don't have the money to afford a dozen and they don't have the strength to break it into a half dozen

TIMMY: I'll have the money

WAYNE: You'll spill the chemicals

TIMMY: I—

WAYNE: Brushing the pool is easy, but you got to have a steady hand to mix the chemicals.

JOHNNY: You do

WAYNE: They got college graduates with chemistry degrees be glad to take a job like that, how you gonna get it
(Pause.)

WAYNE: And when you get old they'll put you on the ward

TIMMY: They're not putting me on any ward

WAYNE: On the ward

TIMMY: Not me

WAYNE: You think they're gonna put the old pool boy on a bed of white towels, give him his own lounge for the rest of his days

TIMMY: They

WAYNE: You got anybody to wheel you around, you got anybody to wipe your mouth…when your arms hurt too much to pick up the pool brush…in the off season you're a goner
(Pause.)

TIMMY: I'll worry about that when the time comes

WAYNE: You better worry about it now. If you wait to worry about it till the time comes, the time's gonna come for sure
(Pause. Timmy starts opening a can of sardines.)

WAYNE: What are you doing

TIMMY: What does it look like I'm doing

WAYNE: I thought we were going to the Rascal House

TIMMY: We'll go when we go. In the meantime I felt like a sardine

WAYNE: You'll spoil your appetite

TIMMY: It bothers Wayne that I'm always okay with a sardine and there's nothing he's always okay with
(Pause.)

WAYNE: You don't want to wind up like that, Timmy. It's a bad way to wind up

TIMMY: How

WAYNE: Old

TIMMY: How else would you wind up

240 men's scenes

WAYNE: You'd wind up before that. Or somebody else would wind you up

TIMMY: I told you that's why he killed the cat, 'cause he saw that cat old and it scared him

WAYNE: I'd be right to be scared. I remember when I went home and saw the old man gettin' old. It really affected me, seein' him like that, thinkin' look at him he's gettin' to be an old man

JOHNNY: What did you do

WAYNE: I didn't go home anymore

JOHNNY: I woulda beat the shit out of him. Now what about this job

TIMMY: I told you

JOHNNY: I'm leaving

WAYNE: Hang around. Have a Coke

(Wayne goes to the fridge.)

JOHNNY: I don't want a Coke

WAYNE: I said have a Coke

JOHNNY: I said I don't want a fuckin' Coke

(Pause. They glare at each other.)

WAYNE: Then have a grape

JOHNNY: You got an apple?

(Wayne tosses Johnny an apple. Johnny takes out a pocketknife and cuts and eats slices.)

JOHNNY: I just want an answer

WAYNE: You'll get an answer

TIMMY: I don't like it, we don't need it

WAYNE: You don't know what we need. What about Cuba

(Pause.)

WAYNE: I said what about Cuba

JOHNNY: What

TIMMY: Wayne, are you nuts

WAYNE: Cuba, that's what we need the stake for

(Timmy jumps on Wayne. Johnny pulls him off.)

JOHNNY: Sore spot?

TIMMY: I don't know what he's talking about

WAYNE: Cuba

TIMMY: Never heard of the place

JOHNNY: I did

TIMMY: What did you hear

JOHNNY: That they don't have any food down there. And you can't find a bar of soap

TIMMY: Right, you're right. Just let's drop it

WAYNE: But they're going to need it when it opens up

TIMMY: Wayne

WAYNE: When Cuba opens up it's gonna be like nothing else. It's gonna be like the Gold Rush and we'll have a 2000 mile head start.

TIMMY: Wayne, for Chrissake

WAYNE: It's gonna be like D-Day and we're gonna be the first ones to hit the beach

TIMMY: Jesus

WAYNE: He's just one guy

TIMMY: But he'll tell one guy

WAYNE: It's the jewel of the Caribbean. When the lights… Timmy…when the lights…

TIMMY: When the lights go on in Cuba they'll go out every place else

JOHNNY: Cuba? Cuba? I'll tell you what I think. I think Cuba ain't all it's cracked up to be. It's nice from far but far from nice.

TIMMY: It is not

JOHNNY: Cuba's like a pussy, all closed up, all hidden away. When you get there you figure you'll be in Heaven, but it's just like all the rest of them, spend a few nights in it you're ready to get back on the ship
    (Pause.)

TIMMY: What's wrong with any of them

JOHNNY: I didn't say anything was wrong

TIMMY: I think you got a problem

JOHNNY: You want to suck on this
    (They face off…)

JOHNNY: Besides, all the Cubans are up here

242 men's scenes

TIMMY: But when Cuba opens up…

JOHNNY: Then the rest will come

WAYNE: See, Timmy, it doesn't matter that I told him, he's too young to understand. are we going to go to the Rascal House and talk about this or…

TIMMY: The line will be too long

JOHNNY: It's four o'clock in the afternoon

TIMMY: The early bird special

JOHNNY: That's you two guys, a coupla old ladies sharing the early bird special

WAYNE: Fuck you

TIMMY: Nothing's wrong with the early bird special. These two ladies at the next table got the early bird special to split. They got a piece of halibut, it was enough for the both of them. They asked me to cut it for them and I did

JOHNNY: While you were reaching in their handbag

TIMMY: It takes two hands to cut a piece of halibut

WAYNE: Are we going to go

TIMMY: I told you, the line

JOHNNY: Who waits in line

TIMMY: At the Rascal House everybody does. Even Meyer Lansky did.

WAYNE: He did not

TIMMY: He did, he had his meetings in line at the Rascal House

WAYNE: He had his meetings in the cafeteria at the Miami Heart Institute

TIMMY: He had his meetings in line at the Rascal House and walking up and down Collins Avenue cars would pull over now and then and he'd exchange a few words

WAYNE: He'd exchange a few words in the aisles of the Publix Market on Alton Road

JOHNNY: You telling me that Meyer Lansky ran Cuba out of the cereal aisle?

WAYNE: Were you there

JOHNNY: Were you
    (Pause.)

WAYNE: We're gonna be the first ones in

JOHNNY: In where

WAYNE: Cuba

TIMMY: We read the headlines, we watch CNN, when it opens up we go in

WAYNE: We drive down to Key West, we clocked it

TIMMY: Three hours

WAYNE: We got a guy with a boat

JOHNNY: And when you get there…they got nothing to steal

WAYNE: Asshole. We're not going to take, we're going to bring. They need everything down there. Nothing's been painted in thirty years, all Havana needs is a good coat of paint and—and with American loans they'll be able to pay…World Bank…Latin American banks…once you got the guarantees in place

JOHNNY: Where are you gonna get the money to buy what you're going to sell them

(Pause.)

JOHNNY: I'll tell you where. These people went to the Heat game and left it for you

TIMMY: What have they left for us

JOHNNY: Jewelry, bearer bonds. It would give you a sweet stake

TIMMY: I'll get it somewhere else

WAYNE: Listen to him, Timmy. It might be what we need

TIMMY: I don't know, I don't know, I don't think I can…not before I go to Cuba, I got to go down there clean. I got to cross the ocean a certain way, I can't bring any of this shit with me. See, sometimes the trip across saltwater is cleansing, you get down there you're a new man

WAYNE: That's what I'm telling you, you do what you gotta do to get your stake, and then you get cleansed

TIMMY: But I want to go down there pure

WAYNE: I'm telling you you're getting cleansed

TIMMY: I want to feel worthy of being cleansed

WAYNE: You fuckin' asshole, the whole point of being cleansed is that you don't feel worthy. That's why you get cleansed

244 men's scenes

JOHNNY: *(To Wayne.)* What's the matter with him

WAYNE: Don't worry about him. He's just a little strange. He suffers from depression

TIMMY: I don't suffer from depression

WAYNE: You don't?

TIMMY: I get depressed

JOHNNY: There's shit you can take for that.

246

by Craig Wright is subject to royalty. It is fully protected under the copyright laws of the United States of America, and of all countries covered by the International Copyright Union (including the Dominion of Canada and the rest of the British Commonwealth), and of all countries covered by the Pan-American Copyright Convention and the Universal Copyright Convention, the Berne Convention and of all countries with which the United States has reciprocal copyright relations. All rights, including professional, amateur/motion picture stage rights, recitation, lecturing, public reading, radio broadcasting, television, video or sound recording, all other forms of mechanical or electrical reproduction, such as CD-ROM, CD-1, information storage and retrieval systems and photocopying, and the rights of translation into foreign languages, are strictly reserved. Particular emphasis is laid upon the matter of readings, permission for which must be obtained from the author's agent in writing. The stage performance rights in MOLLY'S DELICIOUS (other than first class rights) are controlled exclusively by The Dramatic Publishing Company, P.O. Box 129, Woodstock, IL 60098. No professional or non-professional performance of the Play (excluding first class professional performance) may be given without obtaining in advance the written permission of The Dramatic Publishing Company, and paying the requisite fee. Contact: Helen Merrill, Ltd., 425 West 23rd Street, Suite 1F, New York, NY 10011.

THE ORNAMENTAL HERMIT by Jocelyn Beard. Copyright © 1998, by Jocelyn Beard. Reprinted by permission of the author. Contact: Jocelyn Beard, (914) 878-6388.

THE PHARMACIST'S DAUGHTER by Monika Monika. Copyright © 1997, by Monika Monika. Reprinted by permission of Rosenstone/Wender. Contact: Rosenstone/Wender, 3 East 48th Street, New York, NY 10017, (212) 832-8330, Attn: Ronald Gwiazda, Author's Agent.

PLUNGE by Christopher Kyle. Copyright © 1997, by Christopher Kyle. Reprinted by permission of Helen Merrill, Ltd. Contact: Helen Merrill, Ltd., 425 West 23rd Street, 1F, New York, NY 10011.

POLAROID STORIES by Naomi Iizuka. Copyright © 1997, by Naomi Iizuka. Produced by the Actor's Theatre of Louisville. Reprinted by permission of the author. Contact: Helen Merrill, Ltd., 425 West 23rd Street, 1F, New York, NY 10011.

REFRIGERATORS by Judy Soo Hoo. Copyright © 1997, by Judy Soo Hoo. Reprinted by permission of the author. Contact: Judy Soo Hoo, 11550 Nebraska Avenue, #110, Los Angeles, CA 90025.

SCOTLAND ROAD by Jeffrey Hatcher. Copyright © 1996, by Jeffrey Hatcher. CAUTION: Professionals and amateurs are hereby warned that performance of SCOTLAND ROAD by Jeffrey Hatcher is subject to royalty. It is fully protected under the copyright laws of the United States of America, and of all countries covered by the International Copyright Union (including the Dominion of Canada and the rest of the British Commonwealth), and of all countries covered by the Pan-American Copyright Convention and the Universal Copyright Convention, the Berne Convention and of all countries with which the United States has reciprocal copyright relations. All rights, including professional, amateur/motion picture stage rights, recitation, lecturing, public reading, radio broadcasting, television, video or sound recording, all other forms of mechanical or electrical reproduction, such as CD-ROM, CD-1, information storage and retrieval systems and photocopying, and the rights of translation into foreign languages, are strictly reserved. Particular emphasis is laid upon the matter of readings, permission for which must be obtained from the author's agent in writing. The stage performance rights in SCOTLAND ROAD (other than first class rights) are controlled exclusively by the Dramatists Play Service, Inc., 440 Park Avenue

249

South, New York, NY 10016. No professional or non-professional performance of the play (excluding first class professional performance) may be given without obtaining in advance the written permission of the Dramatists Play Service, Inc., and paying the requisite fee. Contact: John Santoianni, c/o The Tantleff Office, 375 Greenwich Avenue, Suite 700, New York, NY 10013.

THE SHIVA QUEEN by Rebecca Ritchie. Copyright © 1997, by Rebecca Ritchie. Reprinted by permission of the author. Contact: Stafford D. Ritchie, Esq., 200 Olympic Towers, 300 Pearl Street, Buffalo, NY 14202.

SODA FOUNTAIN by Richard Lay. Copyright © 1997, by Richard Lay. Reprinted by permission of the author. Contact: Richard Lay, 205 West 15th Street, 2M, New York, NY 10011, (212) 929-3423.

SOUL SURVIVOR by Ted Lange. Copyright © 1998, by Ted Lange, all rights reserved. Reprinted by permission of the author. Contact: Ted Lange, 7420 Corbin Avenue, #17, Reseda, CA 91335.

subCITY by Bob Jude Ferrante. Copyright © 1998, by Bob Jude Ferrante, Reprinted by permission of the author. Contact: Bob Jude Ferrante, 616 East 19th Street, Brooklyn, NY 11230.

SVETLANA'S NEW FLAME by Olga Humphrey. Copyright © 1997, by Olga Humphrey. Reprinted by permission of Helen Merrill, Ltd. CAUTION: Professionals and amateurs are hereby warned that performance of SVETLANA'S NEW FLAME by Olga Humphrey is subject to royalty. It is fully protected under the copyright laws of the United States of America, and of all countries covered by the International Copyright Union (including the Dominion of Canada and the rest of the British Commonwealth), and of all countries covered by the Pan-American Copyright Convention and the Universal Copyright Convention, the Berne Convention and of all countries with which the United States has reciprocal copyright relations. All rights, including professional, amateur/motion picture stage rights, recitation, lecturing, public reading, radio broadcasting, television, video or sound recording, all other forms of mechanical or electrical reproduction, such as CD-ROM, CD-1, information storage and retrieval systems and photocopying, and the rights of translation into foreign languages, are strictly reserved. Particular emphasis is laid upon the matter of readings, permission for which must be obtained from the author's agent in writing. The stage performance rights in SVETLANA'S NEW FLAME are controlled exclusively by Helen Merrill, Ltd. No professional or non-professional performance of the play may be given without obtaining in advance the written permission of Helen Merrill, Ltd. and paying the requisite fee. Contact: Helen Merrill, Ltd., 425 West 23rd Street, Suite 1F, New York, NY 10011.

THREE DAYS OF RAIN by Richard Greenberg. Copyright © 1997, by Richard Greenberg. Reprinted by permission of the author. CAUTION: Professionals and amateurs are hereby warned that performance of THREE DAYS OF RAIN by Richard Greenberg is subject to royalty. It is fully protected under the copyright laws of the United States of America, and of all countries covered by the International Copyright Union (including the Dominion of Canada and the rest of the British Commonwealth), and of all countries covered by the Pan-American Copyright Convention and the Universal Copyright Convention, the Berne Convention and of all countries with which the United States has reciprocal copyright relations. All rights, including professional, amateur/motion picture stage rights, recitation, lecturing, public reading, radio broadcasting, television, video or sound recording, all other forms of mechanical or electrical reproduction, such as CD-ROM, CD-1, information stor-

Smith and Kraus *Books For Actors*
SCENE STUDY SERIES
Scenes From Classic Plays 468 B.C. to 1960 A.D.
The Best Stage Scenes of 1996
The Best Stage Scenes of 1995
The Best Stage Scenes of 1994
The Best Stage Scenes of 1993
The Best Stage Scenes of 1992
The Best Stage Scenes for Men / Women from the 1980s
THE MONOLOGUE SERIES
The Ultimate Audition Book: 200 Monologuess, 2 Minutes & Under
The Best Men's / Women's Stage Monologues of 1997
The Best Men's / Women's Stage Monologues of 1996
The Best Men's / Women's Stage Monologues of 1995
The Best Men's / Women's Stage Monologues of 1994
The Best Men's / Women's Stage Monologues of 1993
The Best Men's / Women's Stage Monologues of 1992
The Best Men's / Women's Stage Monologues of 1991
The Best Men's / Women's Stage Monologues of 1990
One Hundred Men's / Women's Stage Monologues from the 1980s
2 Minutes and Under: Character Monologues for Actors
Street Talk: Character Monologues for Actors
Uptown: Character Monologues for Actors
Ice Babies in Oz: Character Monologues for Actors
Monologues from Contemporary Literature: Volume I
Monologues from Classic Plays
100 Great Monologues from the Renaissance Theatre
100 Great Monologues from the Neo-Classical Theatre
100 Great Monologues from the 19th C. Romantic and Realistic Theatres
A Brave and Violent Theatre: 20th C. Irish Monologues, Scenes & Historical
    Context
Kiss and Tell: Restoration Monologues, Scenes and Historical Context
The Great Monologues from the Humana Festival
The Great Monologues from the EST Marathon
The Great Monologues from the Women's Project
The Great Monologues from the Mark Taper Forum
YOUNG ACTOR SERIES
Great Scenes and Monologues for Children
Great Monologues for Young Actors, Vol.1 and Vol.2
Great Scenes for Young Actors, Vol.1 and Vol.2
Multicultural Monologues for Young Actors
Multicultural Scenes for Young Actors

If you require pre-publication information about upcoming Smith and Kraus
books, you may receive our semi-annual catalogue, free of charge, by sending
your name and address to *Smith and Kraus Catalogue, P.O. Box 127, Lyme, NH
03768. Or call us at (603) 922-5118, fax (603) 922-3348.*